When Did
YOU
Die?

What People Are Saying About Temple Hayes

"Truth pours forth here to wake you up to what it means to be truly alive and fully in your body. This compelling and life-changing book will make you feel exhilarated. I want everyone to read it."

—**Donna Eden**,
author of *The Energies of Love*
and *Energy Medicine*

"Temple Hayes is a catalyst for total transformation."

—**Janet Bray Attwood**,
New York Times bestselling author,
The Passion Test

"Magnetizing, energizing, and inspiring . . . remembering who you were born to be. Read *When Did You Die?* knowing your life is about to change in a profound way."

—**Dennis Merritt Jones**
Author of *Your (Re)Defining Moments—*
Becoming Who You Were Born to Be

"Temple Hayes is a powerful, dynamic leader of change . . . Her book *When Did You Die?* is designed to bring about important changes in the way we think and relate to the world. We keep our true selves under wraps for much of our lives—now this book will bring us out."

—**Caroline Sutherland**
author of *The Body Knows . . .*
How to Stay Young

"One of the brightest lights in the spiritual movement today . . . a clear beacon for people who want to express more of their authentic selves and reach their highest potential."

—**Noah St. John**
author of *The Book of Afformations*

"*When Did You Die?* will open hearts and minds around the world. When Temple has a vision, she makes it happen!"

—**Deborah King**
Hay House radio host, author of
Be Your Own Shaman and *Truth Heals*

"Very few of today's spiritual leaders can deliver a message like Temple Hayes. Yet again in *When Did You Die?* she connects with people on the deepest levels, moving beyond the time of their emotional death and giving them a chance to be reborn!"

Michelle Phillips
TV and radio host, speaker, and bestselling author of
The Beauty Blueprint: 8 Steps to Building the Life and Look of Your Dreams

"A new book by Temple Hayes is cause for celebration. The world is a better place with Temple in it, and now even more souls will be enlightened by her beautiful spirit."

Suzanne Giesemann
Author of *Messages of Hope* and *Wolf's Message*

When Did YOU *Die?*

8 Steps to Stop Dying Every Day and START Waking Up!

Temple Hayes

Health Communications, Inc.
Deerfield Beach, Florida

www.hcibooks.com

Permission Note: "A Ritual for the Path of My Faith," From *Practicing the Presence of the Goddess* (New World Library, 2000) by Doctor Barbara Ardinger (www.barbaraardinger.com). Published with permission.

Cataloging-in-Publication Data is available through the Library of Congress

ISBN-13: 978-0-7573-1810-8 (paperback)
ISBN-10: 0-7573-1810-X (paperback)
ISBN-13: 978-0-7573-1811-5 (ePub)
ISBN-10: 0-7573-1811-8 (ePub)

Publisher: Health Communications, Inc.
         3201 S.W. 15th Street
         Deerfield Beach, FL 33442–8190

Cover, interior design, and formatting by Lawna Patterson Oldfield

*I dedicate this book to the
deep appreciation of life, for when the
awakened door truly opens, there is no life
that can be overlooked or not immensely valued.
Every life matters—all life, not only
people but all living things.*

CONTENTS

ACKNOWLEDGMENTS

To my parents, for birthing me many, many times.

To my Creator, for creating me and allowing me the freedom to create myself.

To BB, Barbara Bertucci, who as my life partner taught me how to love and blessed me.

To my healers and teachers—Berenice Andrews, Guruji Sri Sri Poonamji, and Marilyn Gail Rodack—who revealed to me how to live.

To Minx Boren, who gave friendship a new definition and changed me forever.

To Unity, my spiritual community, which saved my life.

To New Thought and Centers for Spiritual Living, who gave me a place to play.

To First Unity of St. Petersburg, Florida, who gave me a space to evolve my knowing, growing, and showing.

To Judy Reardon, who said no to my alcohol and yes to my life—a true friend.

To Carl and Marilyn Weiss and Richard and Audrey Frederick, part of my forever beloved community.

To Carol D'Alessandro and Sharon Lardieri, whose wellspring of love and family never runs dry.

To Bernice Novack, Tom West, Bill Gove, and Alice Lowry Corby, my confidants for many years who have walked into their next lives.

To Celeste McShane, a dear friend and supporter.

To Linda Morris, my mastermind partner for almost twenty years.

To LouAnne Saraga Walters, for her support with *How to Speak Unity* and for her passion for *When Did You Die?*

To Carmen Matos and Bill Matos, my other chosen family.

To Rebecca Johnson, who nudged me forward to be a writer and supported me with Life Rights and introduced me to JoAnn Deck.

To Health Communications, Inc., for seizing the opportunity to support my work, with special thanks to Allison Janse and Kim Weiss.

To Suzanne Giesemann, my great colleague and confidante.

To Claudette and Stephanie Michaud, my tribal, energetic friends.

To Dennis Merritt Jones, my spiritual brother.

To JoAnn Deck, my incredible literary agent.

To Sir Digby—whom I loved beyond words and who died during this writing, thus opening up a deepening of my heart—and all my four-footed furry family.

To Don and Peggy Sandin (my astrologer) and Riley.

To John Bergstrom, my E3 (eternally, endlessly, effortlessly) friend who named me the Feather Lady.

To Sandi Hulon, Sean Michael Davis, Lynda Lyday, and Jen Burkley-Cudar, for their energy.

To Carol and Igor Gruendl, Josie Barber, Lorri Franckle, and Dianna Collins, my inner circle.

To Nelson and Tracy Hayes, John and Miranda Hayes, and family near and dear to me.

To Kim Brown Harrelson, my beloved friend all my life since age three.

To my relatives, the Councils, for your love and acceptance.

To Beverly Alberstadt Bartholow, my 111 angel (our sacred heart code), my eternal friend.

To Andrea Dudley, my sacred supporter.

To Dea Shandera-Hunter and Brent Hunter, lights in the West.

To all the many sacred teachers, congregants, and friends in my life, kind and unkind, who have touched me beyond measure.

INTRODUCTION

When Did You Die?
How to Recognize When You're Dying a Bit Every Day

The secret of life is not whether we will live or die;
it is the parts of ourselves which we allow
to die while we are living.

—**Gary Busey**, Hollywood actor, who was given
this message when he had a near-death
experience in a motorcycle accident

We are walking our path in paradoxical times. We hear that the world is waking up, yet we read every day that another life or many lives have been taken by senseless tragedies. We evolve with technology yet ponder how to stay connected. We have prepackaged foods yet struggle to take care of ourselves. We have more knowledge but seem to know less. We believe in dreams yet have difficulty believing in our own. We long to believe in God or something larger than ourselves, yet we do not seem to understand that the way to God is by loving what is closest to us.

We have more wealth, yet in so many ways we are still poor, and many of us are longing for a life of meaning, value, and purpose. We long to have a message and an understanding of life that allows us to be heard, recognized, and discovered for who we truly are. We long to matter, and as a teacher of mine many years ago always said, "We are here not to solve all the problems of the world but to not be one of the problems of the world."

We have become a "me" or "what about me" generation, yet we do not innately understand that there is not a true *me* expressing in most of us. We are programmed and robotic rather than innately being who we are destined to be.

All of us long to be appreciated and valued. We long to be seen and heard. Until we see and hear our own inner voices and callings, we will simply continue to die a little each and every day.

I wrote this book because I have come to understand that our experiences and challenges play a major role in our development. I am the same person now that I was at five years old—a person who "survived myself" long enough to understand the difference between our earthly birth story and the magic and miracles of our sacred creation story. I understood that embracing my Creator offered me the crayons for the amazing coloring book of my own life. I somehow finally understood that the anger and disconnected feelings I had carried most of my life really weren't anger with and disconnection from the Creator but were anger with and disconnection from myself.

The only difference between who I was then and who I am now is that I have given myself total permission to be vulnerable and real and not be concerned with what someone else thinks of me. I believe I was born to write this book, and from my living a little and dying a little (a lot of dying a little, actually), I have become more awake and a little wiser. I believe that life is simple but that because of our inability to see how natural our paths are destined to be, we have made life hard and complicated.

We are living in a time in our society when we need to move beyond scratching the surface by sharing platitudes and clichés and bumper sticker truths. We need teachings of depth and practical applications to show us how we can die many times in a lifetime and how, with our permission and willingness to do so, we can stop dying all these times and truly live. We all long to become fully present and alive. It is our true sacred creation story.

We often fear or avoid the call of death within our lifetimes, hoping that science will create a magic pill or potion so that we will not have to exit this go-round. Death will be our ultimate gift to the life we have lived. We can deny it, yet the key secret to life—the magic code—is realizing that being born and dying are not once-in-a-lifetime events.

We actually choose life or death on a daily basis. And while we are determined to avoid aging and avoid the truth that we will die, we miss out on the greatest performance of all time: *not dying while we are living.*

In this book you will learn how to choose life over death every day. You will learn to wake up, to celebrate your life, and feel the excitement you were born to express.

The Many Layers of Dying a Bit Every Day

Many people do not realize that there are many layers of being asleep and dying while we are living. We are so caught up in the motions of living, eating, working, and making and keeping appointments that we don't realize that we died to our potential a long time ago. We have become robotic! How do you know whether you've been dying a bit every day? One key way is to notice if you are feeling disconnected or drained rather than energized or impassioned about your life. Listed below are a number of life events which can happen to us and we lose energy in our bodies if we have not spiritually or emotionally handled them to find a sense of peace. Please take some time to evaluate real moments in your life and consider the questions below to see which ones apply to your current situation:

- Have you ever been involved in an automobile or a motorcycle accident? Have you had another type of major accident or life-threatening condition?
- Have you ever lost a loved one from death or separation and you are not completely at peace with it?
- Have you ever had major surgery?
- Are you carrying a dream that is not currently being fulfilled?
- Do you explain, justify, or defend yourself at least once a week?
- Have you ever had, or do you currently have, an addiction?
- Do you have sugar and/or carbohydrate cravings?
- Do half the clothes in your closet either not fit you or not appeal to you?
- Do you long for something more in life?
- Are you in an unhappy relationship or marriage?
- Do you feel not seen or heard by a number of people in your life?
- Do you have what feels like endless days during which you feel sad and anxious?
- Is your energy level not what it used to be?
- Are you waiting for something to happen so you can then be happy?
- Do you have people in your life who you know do not deserve to be there?
- Within the past twenty-four hours, have you had an encounter with someone to whom you did not say what you truly felt or wanted to say?

If you answered yes to two or more of these questions, then you are a person who has been dying a bit every day. Because you've picked up this book, you are obviously ready to benefit from these writings.

You have the potential to become more alive, more authentic, more youthful, and more energetic. I know it, and deep down you know it, too. Subtle deaths on a daily basis are just as significant as the larger ones. They add up a bit every day and take away our life force, our creativity, and our energy. Subtle deaths prevent us from experiencing the miracles and magic that are our birthright.

We are not designed to grow *old*; we are created to grow *up* and *out* as beings of light. Some would call this the lightness of being or taking yourself lightly. Whether or not you believe in the Bible, when the Creator said, "Let there be light," the Creator was talking about you. Even Jesus tells a parable in which he reminds us not to hide our light. We are that light, and, as long as we hide it, we are hiding from ourselves. We are dying a little rather than thriving a lot. As long as we stand in the way of our light rather than expressing as a sparkle, we are merely a shadow of who we could be.

My Mission to You

I'm going to show you how to stop dying a bit every day and start seeing yourself as someone who can be fully awake to your complete and present life. No matter what your background, no matter what you have gone through in life, you and I are going to transform all that, and, once you stop dying a little bit every day, you will begin to see yourself as the empowered being that you are, worthy of love and happiness and being fully alive. You will shift from being disconnected and drained to being energized and impassioned.

When you learn more about my life—the pain, the rejection, the dismissal by many—some of you may be surprised that I hold on to God in a way that is not only a choice but also a necessity. I believe that having a relationship with our divine Creator is absolutely necessary to have a thriving and vibrant life. I want to share with you how I started seeing life from a new perspective by understanding in depth that we cannot separate ourselves from the very essence that we are made of.

We can deny it or pretend that it doesn't exist, the way some people attempt to separate from their birth mothers. We can dislike, distrust, and separate from our birth parents and pretend there is no connection whatsoever, yet we will still have qualities like them. We will do things a certain way and wonder why we do it; we will have memories or intuitive moments and feel something worth pondering. We can separate ourselves from our family of origin, even move to a different country to be away from our family members, yet there will still be characteristics of them within us. We may deny them, yet we should never want to deny the gratitude we have because through these people we were given life.

On a much grander scale, who birthed us (our earthly story) is small compared to our sacred story (our creation story), which we should recognize and honor. Until we connect with our creation story and recognize the Creator who has given us life, we will be incapable of truly living and being born into our magnificent selves.

Being angry and disconnected from the Creator who gave you life is like having a parent who, unbeknownst to you, is very, very rich. You have denied yourself a relationship with this parent all your life, and one day you realize that you could have inherited amazing riches had you been willing to open your heart. Our Creator has given each of us amazing riches, gifts, and talents, but only when we seek to be open to the kingdom of the riches will they be ours for the taking.

Living life without deepening an appreciation of the Creator who gave you life is like having a beautiful coloring book and carrying it around all your life, yet you have no crayons to color with and so you cannot truly see what an awesome gift you are toting from place to place. Denying our creation story and cutting ourselves off from the flow of our Creator is like having a large chest filled with magic and wonder that we carry everywhere but have never opened; we have not honored where it came from enough to even be motivated to find the key. The key to an energized life is the ability to understand with deep honor and reverence both our earthly story and our sacred story. As I look back, I see that God and I have been connected for a very long time.

I can still feel the image in my heart and the uncertainty I had as a five-year-old girl sitting in a tree and hearing a voice say to me, "One day you will share a message the world will want to hear." God spoke to me all the time, but no one in my earthly story believed me when I told them that.

One of the first memories I have of becoming aware of my ability to use the gifts my Creator gave me occurred when I was seven years old. It was very important for me to have a dog. Now that I look back, I can see that this was an expression of my deep appreciation and understanding of nature. I seemed to always understand that there is more to life than what we see. I seemed to just know that I could think and feel things into my life. There was an innate reality within me that understood that just as there is an abundance of everything within nature, there is equally an abundance available to us. Somehow I knew that nature is our way of experiencing God. I also knew that the creations of nature offer unconditional love, and, because I was not feeling it in my household, I was seeking it from a pet. Pets offer us spiritual medicine and bring to us the energy we need at the time.

My parents were no different from many folks at the time who thought that a dog, a cat, or any other animal was a waste of time and just one more thing to tend to. It was clear that no one else in my family seemed to understand that for me a pet was crucial to my well-being. I needed something I could relate to that offered me daily God-blessings of love that were tangible, and I knew a dog could give it to me. I was already wounded from the environment I lived in, from the arguing and the rage, and living in daily fear of what was going to happen to us with a dysfunctional father and an abused mother. A dog could help me heal. I was dying a little from a lack of nurturing, and I needed unconditional interaction with a pet. I begged for a dog, I cried for a dog, and yet my parents were sure that I would not take care of it. There were two answers: "No" and "Because I said so." How could they know I would not take care of a dog if I was never given a chance?

The answer is that they projected themselves onto me. They were assuming that I would not take care of a pet because they were not taking care of me. I was dying inside, for no one could truly see me— the gifted one!

I decided I would go over their heads and go directly to my source of nature. I stopped asking them and began to pray to God, my Creator, who I knew deep inside spoke to me all the time. Within a few weeks, a beautiful stray dog showed up at my doorstep. Even though I had heard God speaking to me while I was in nature when I was five years old, and I had always felt such a strong relationship, witnessing my request being answered so directly showed me how connected I really was. Until this event of manifesting my dog, I had not totally connected the dots. It was this defining moment that revealed to me that I could "call in" and pray for what I wanted, and it would be granted. I realized at this moment that I was connected to something greater than myself, and the reason I desired life-affirming experiences is because they were mine to have. I could see clearly that a prayer for a desire wasn't a new, unheard-of plea to the God who made me; a prayer from me to God was letting God know I had heard the desire and I was saying yes.

The secret to life is not in learning new formulas to have the life you long to have. The secret to life is to embody your sacred creation story. You are here to bring your message to our planet, and, when you truly understand this, all you need in order to bring this message to this life will be given to you. You were born with all the innate gifts you need to be rich, healthy, and happy. Most important, you are here to bring the message of your life to our planet; when you truly realize this, all you need in order to bring the message of your life to this life will be given to you.

Creating a New Paradigm

Sometimes it seems that out of fear and insecurity, a number of traditional philosophies do not want us to understand how easy it is for us to manifest our desires. The original sacred texts clearly taught us that we were here to live a life of miracles and magic and share our original message with our world. There were mystery schools that supported individuals to come into their own. Yet controlling and man-made philosophies did away with the ancient teachings so that people could be guided, directed, manipulated, and controlled.

We are not commonly raised to be independent thinkers and creators of our own destiny. I was taught that I could not go directly to God with my desires because he was too busy up there keeping up with all our shortcomings, but I did not resonate with this way of thinking. I knew this was a lie, although I did not dare to share it because no one else around me was open to the idea. Oh, I attempted to, a time or two along the way, but I was treated so oddly that I became a chameleon.

As long as people live by the old paradigm of using formulas that are human-made rather than ordained by Spirit, they will never be fully present to live an empowered life. It is natural for us to live intuitively and create a wonderfully rich and rewarding life. The challenge is that it is unnatural for us to live according to what other people tell us: our parents, guardians, teachers, and doctors. Once people cross the line of unnaturally being told what to do and what to be, they begin to die a little, and many never again create a new paradigm by which to live innately in the way they were designed and destined.

It is as if many people have become robots and outside sources are trying to create one remote control to operate all of us. The remote control consists of twenty-four-hour biased news, medical advertisements 24/7, and pretentious role models making millions telling people how to do something they have never done themselves. The situation has gotten way out of hand, and my purpose as a spiritual leader is to urge everyone to take a time-out and realize we are getting worse rather than better. We know more than ever, yet we are showing very little of what we know. As a world we have become weary, for we have lessened our energy by the day-to-day lack of celebrating this amazing life.

We get better by admitting, first and foremost, that we as a world are ready for help. We get better by understanding that a few simple causes have made us get worse. We get better by realizing that it will not take a lot to get us where we need to be. We get better by being willing to know better and by directing this energy into doing better.

We get better by realizing that we have more information available to us than we have ever had, yet first we must realize that many of us seem to be more ignorant than we have ever been. Knowing a fact doesn't mean anything unless our knowing transforms into our growing, then transcends us into our showing.

We get better by showing everything and everyone around us that indeed we are growing. We are knowing, growing, and showing our divine possibilities by learning to live as authentic, empowered individuals rather than attempting to be one size that fits all, governed by one remote control.

I saw early in my life how easy it was for people in my school, my neighborhood, and my town to die a little and sometimes a lot. I saw how most people around me lived their lives believing only what their families said, or their doctors or their teachers, and never experimenting beyond those walls of limitation to see what their Creator had in mind and in store for them. Most of the people I met as a child lived from the outside in rather than from the inside out.

All amazing human beings come to understand that there is a forked path in life: the path of familiarity (our families, our earthly story) and the original and unique path of our destiny (our sacred lives, our creation story). The path on which we will be awake and fully alive is as unique as our fingerprints. There is no one else who can walk it or be on it for us.

Those of you who are feeling as if you are dying a bit every day, I understand. I died a lot before I was a teenager. You are not dying because it's too hard to be you, however. You are dying because you are *not* being you; that's what makes life hard.

By the time I was fourteen years old, I was already dying. I became a regular customer at one particular aisle at my local grocery store. That aisle had one item, alcohol, though many different brands. It was the aisle I would go to last, once all the other shopping was done, in order to numb myself one more time while I participated in not being fully alive. Of course, at this age someone older had to go with me and help me purchase items from Aisle 13. This was the isle where I grew up. It was an unlucky aisle for me from the very beginning; it offered a way for the gifted, the unheard, and the unseen to not feel the pain of dying.

Alcohol used to be the legal drug to numb ourselves with. For you younger readers, it's now much easier to get all sorts of drugs that will make you forget how to spell your middle name or count to ten. Who ever dreamed we could go to a certified medical practitioner and get a prescription for a pill that would allow us to be asleep daily or to sleep because we are not living lives of our own making?

This book is my story of how I have lived, died, and been reborn many times. This is my story of how I lived long enough to discover how my stories of "woundology" would later become my sacred creation stories and transform my life to the true me. It has been an amazing, fascinating, and ongoing journey. I learned that we are not made to be old in spirit; we are birthed for our spirit to remain forever young, and the more years that are added to our lives, the more light we will have to give.

We have all met many young people who seem old beyond their years because they have already begun to die a little every day, and their light has been diminished. The distinction is to understand that spiritually we all age, but, at the same time, aging without being old is not only possible, it is natural.

Your light is your energy, your gift to the world. And your lightness of being is your gift to yourself. Making a decision to stop dying will greatly increase your capacity to start living and to manifest your true purpose in life. You will now begin to shine.

❧ 1 ❧

Time to Wake Up

Step One: How to Put Your Whole Self into Your Life

The vibrancy of life is all around us. Nature is continuously giving of itself in order for us to be energized and impassioned yet we must wake up. We are created to be vibrant beings.

Would you say that you have felt somewhat disconnected and drained? Do you often feel like life is not giving you the joy, passion, and drive you felt when you were a child? Have you ever felt like you awoke from a dream that wouldn't let you go even though you knew you had woken up? Welcome to the journey that most people consider a normal part of being human. However, the inner cause of feeling disconnected and drained is that our society and surroundings often do not allow us the chance to be our true selves. We often approach life being half awake, which gets in the way of our success. True success is measured by how we thrive and live being totally alive, rather than being drained and weary.

It is without a doubt time to wake up!

I was thirty-eight years old when a life of subtle deaths started to catch up with me. I had already been successful in the corporate world. I had been successful in the sales world. I had succeeded as an athlete (batting average .616, selected as an All-American Softball Player in 1979) and was physically in great shape. I had served my country in the U.S. Army Reserves and been sober for nine years. I had loved and been loved, and I could share at gatherings that I have had the same best friend since I was three years old. I had been going to therapy since I was thirty and could tell you a lot of information about the family system, the inner child, "woundology," and how to no longer be dysfunctional. I had begun to understand quite well why I was dying a little, and I had become successful so that no one would know I was dying inside, but I desperately needed help.

You could say that on the outside I appeared to have a lot going for me, but on the inside something was deeply missing. I felt as if I were dying. I could only describe it to myself as a soul ache. More than words, this subtle dying was a feeling or a sense, like a weighted-down plant with dead leaves and branches. I felt strained and often numb in my day-to-day existence.

I needed someone to be awake enough to see that even though I had changed my world, my world was not really changing. I needed someone who could see that deep down, beneath all the trophies, successes, brightness, and accolades, I needed help. I needed something or someone to help me wake up. I needed to come back to living, yet I simply did not know how.

I had always had a lot of energy and zest for life, but the colors of the rainbow were fading, and I was feeling more and more depleted of the enthusiasm to keep going. The drive that had been getting me up, getting me out, and enabling me to show up was burning out.

Even though I was connecting inside myself, I knew I was not home. I could not find me.

The following is one of my favorite stories: A telemarketer called a household, and the voice on the other end whispered, "Hello." The telemarketer said, "May I speak to the woman of the house, please?" And the voice on the other end of the phone said softly, "She's busy." So the telemarketer said, "Well, can I speak to the man of the house?" The voice on the other end whispered, "He's busy, too!"

"Oh my," stated the caller, "I can hear them talking."

"Yes," said the other person. "They are talking to the fireman."

"Well, let me speak to the fireman," said the caller.

"No, you can't!" stated the other person. "He is talking to the policeman."

"What in the world is going on?" said the telemarketer. "Get someone to the phone!"

"They are looking for me," said the person, who turned out to be a little girl.

This is exactly how I felt. I felt as if I were looking for me and I longed to be found. I felt almost invisible to the world and those around me, and I began to pray to be found.

When we become awake to the ways in which we have died a little, when we become aware of the ways in which we have settled just a little or perhaps a lot, when we realize the ways we have not been our own bus driver, then we can change our experiences immediately. It is like the old axiom: When I do not change circumstances, circumstances change me.

Once we begin to tell ourselves the truth about life, death, and dying, bit by bit we are awakening our heart and mind. A trained mind creates an open heart, yet I had spent my entire life training my mind not to feel my heart. I had been wearing an invisible straitjacket for a very long time. If I don't feel, I believed, I won't reveal myself, and therefore no one and nothing can hurt or reject me.

Once we admit that our worlds are not changing and we need help, we are calling on someone to help us. We are praying for someone to find us. We are longing for our hearts to open.

You Have to Put Your Whole Self In

When I heard the voice at age five that told me I was going to bring a message to the world, I asked the Creator, "What does that mean?" I have spent many years of my life pondering what it meant and longing to understand the meaning of the message I was to deliver.

One day I understood. I was here to teach people about life. I had lived and died many times in this lifetime, so I could speak from my experiences. I had been born a radiant and phenomenal human being, and my light had faded, so I would be able to use these experiences to see where many other people's lights had faded.

Many people have said throughout my lifetime that I was so fortunate to receive this message at an early age. That might be true if my parents had been elders of a tribe, leaders of a mystery school, or sages. But where I lived and I grew up, if you tell people you've heard a voice, they might have put you away. There were moments when I was actually concerned that they would.

I always asked questions and irritated a lot of people because I didn't understand why we did certain things or believed in certain dogmatic ideas. I asked my mother many times in my early years if I was adopted because I just felt so unique and different from the rest of my family. By the time I was forty I was still asking, and she still told me no.

In the early years of my life I realized I could see the energy of people and how they weren't connected, not only to one another but also to themselves. I could always sense whether they were telling the truth or lying. I could tell whether they were actually living or really just dying while they were living. I was so shocked as a child to witness how many people did not think for themselves, how many people were not happy, and how many people were just plain old—not in age, but in their way of being, long before their time.

They were dying. Their life force was barely present, and at times they looked ashen and gray. Have you ever seen the way a person looks in the last phase of cancer, just before dying, or right after having a heart attack? This is the way a lot of people in our society look energetically, and they haven't had a life-threatening condition. They have, however, had a condition that is threatening their lives: a condition called never living. Their light is fading because their bulb is the wrong wattage; it was not designed to be so small but was destined to be much brighter.

In my environment as a child I could also feel the energy and anxiety of animals. We had cows, goats, horses, cats, and dogs in my community. I never knew why I could feel or sense what they were thinking or feeling. For years people told me that animals did not have feelings, but I knew they were wrong. My response was always "If animals do not have feelings, then why do they tremble and why do they run? If animals do not have feelings, then why do they cry or whimper or have sad eyes?" That animals do not have feelings is just a lame excuse that humanity has told itself for years, and one day we will have to apologize to them for being oblivious to what they really are.

I recall a story told to me by my ministerial colleague about her daughter's dog named Cooper. Cooper was the family dog, a Labrador retriever, who deeply loved his yellow tennis ball. Everyone through the years knew this. Cooper would not give up his ball.

When the family cat became ill and died they decided to bury her in the backyard. They dug a deep hole and right after they put the cat into the space, Cooper dropped his ball and left it in the grave.

After I had become a practicing shaman, I was asked to do a soul retrieval on a horse. Soul retrieval is a process for healing and supporting energy in a person or an animal who has suffered trauma, tragedy, or loss and is emotionally fragmented as a result. Soul retrieval restores, renews, and invigorates the individual or life.

This horse was under two years old, and no matter how much the new owners followed the instructions in their horse manual, they could not get the horse to move forward with a steady gait. They would watch her day after day, hesitating to move forward. I agreed to work with her, and I asked to be the only one in her stable.

I walked up to this beautiful horse and told her I was sorry that no one had understood her. I told her that this was the day her life was going to change and that now she could feel safe and validated. As I spoke to her, tears ran from her eyes. With animals as with people, if you attempt to "fix" them without their permission, your chances of success are slim to none.

I laid my hand on her back, and I could see the time of her birth. I could see that she had been a breech birth, that she had been forced out too quickly from her mother, and that it had emotionally affected her. I saw how rather than give her time to heal, her owners at the time had whipped her in the face time and time again to force her to move forward. She had been beaten many times, and she had scars between her eyes. I asked her to forgive us for our ignorance. I assured her that the situation was different now and she could move forward in her life. After this, the new owners felt they would no longer have trouble getting her to move forward. She was energized and felt safe to trust those around her.

I was so elated to be part of such an awakening and renewal of life that I missed the other part of the message until I told my shaman teacher about it. She reminded me that I was a breech birth, that my mother had been in labor forty-eight hours. I, too, had had a forced birth, and in my rebirth I had witnessed how my shoulder was hurt from the force. And I had been beaten many times for my fear of moving forward, not physically but emotionally.

We all need to be seen, validated, and recognized. We need to step back into our innate gifts to inwardly listen to all living things.

I am so grateful that I have lived long enough to finally experience that some people actually believe me now. I have also lived long enough to realize that it does not matter if, because of their ignorance, some people cannot believe me. I know that all living things should have inalienable rights and the freedom to live as they are innately destined. I know that we can no longer destroy nature by taking innocent lives. I know that animals are necessary to our development and that they have feelings and emotions. I know this is true. The children of the twenty-first century innately know this, and they will make a difference in how we treat animal life as long as we do not train their young brains and hearts to believe otherwise.

As I have validated and forgiven myself over the years for taking my life for granted, my gifts are awake again. I had closed these gifts off for many years, and I am so grateful that they have started to come back into my energy field again. Like many of you, I was born a healer, but first I had to die so I could be born again, heal myself, and claim my gifts as a healer.

In my work of healing people and animals, I find that working with animals and children is easier than working with adults, for children and animals are more receptive and do not seek to defend their positions of reality as adults do. Adults will defend their beliefs, habits, and philosophies even though their lives aren't working. I know because I was one of them for a long time, until I discovered my inner spiritual awakening.

We all have the gifts to connect to other living things. We all have the ability to be part of changing someone's world by inner listening and outward validation, yet it requires us to be coming from a trained mind and an open heart.

How Do We Come from an Open Heart?

Do you remember being a little kid and dancing to the song "The Hokey Pokey," putting different parts of yourself into it and then being asked to "put your whole self in"? Remember how good it felt to shake your body and turn around? You were present, alive, and awake! Isn't that what life is all about?

You put your whole self in! This really *is* what life is all about, but why do so few of us put our whole selves in? Most of us in Western culture are not treated as whole and honored from the moment we are born. We are treated like little people with something missing. In certain Eastern traditions, children like myself would have been identified, recognized, and sent to the mystery schools, but in our culture bright children are sent to schools that are themselves a mystery to us, for our educational system does not address our innate and natural gifts. Instead it fills us with knowledge, based on the premise that we are getting something that is missing. We act out or overachieve, for we are not being nurtured and fed in the place where we are already whole. We start out in life as a great big question mark and graduate from school with a degree and a great big period at the end: "Because I said so—period!" "Don't ask any more questions; just do what the boss says—period!" "Just take the pills and do as I say—period!"

We try to be successful according to the textbook rather than following our own inner wisdom and sacred texts.

I've always resonated with these words of Carl Jung, stated in *Memories, Dreams, and Reflections*:

My life often seemed to me like a story that has no beginning and no end. I had the feeling that I was a historical fragment, an excerpt for which the preceding and succeeding text was missing. I could well imagine that I might have lived in former centuries and there encountered questions I was not yet able to answer; that I had been born again because I had not fulfilled the task given to me.

I have been doing christening ceremonies for the past twenty-three years, and each time I invite everyone from the immediate "village," who are there to support the child to come into a circle. I always ask, "What do you wish and pray for with this child?"

The answers come quickly: to live his dreams, to have self-esteem, to believe in herself, to have faith, to feel connected and loved. And so I tell them the following: Then you have to be what you have wished for. This child will mirror you, so if you live in fear, he will live in fear. If you live in lack, she will live in lack. If you are numb, he will be numb. If you pretend to be something you are not, she will pretend to be something she is not. If you doubt the Universe, he will doubt the Universe. If you do not connect with your Creator, she will not feel free to be created. If you teach him that life is designed to be dying while you are living, he will begin to die while he is living. If you are disconnected and drained, then she will be disconnected and drained.

If you live impassioned and energized, then he will live impassioned and energized. If you believe and practice being original, then she will believe and respect being original. If you learn from your lessons when you make a mistake, then he will learn it is okay to make a mistake and not believe that *he* is a mistake. If you show your light rather than a lamp that is broken, then she will shine her light as a lamp to the world.

When we live from a place of wholeness, then we are not experiencing life through the eyes of lack. Therefore, we can give freely of our time, our talent, and our love, for we know that the more we give, the more we will have to give. When we live from a place of wholeness, then others will want to mirror our vibrancy of life. We are forever young. We are difference makers. We are energized.

I can remember as a teenager waiting all summer to return to school in the fall to see whether someone I had a crush on liked me. As we get older, we realize the value of time and become clear about our intentions, and we want to know right away, "Do you like me or not?" Is this something into which we put our whole selves or not? Many people are living life with the brakes on; they are living life in reserve. I have heard many people I have counseled through the years say, "Well, I like him [or her], but I am not going to tell or show him [or her] until I see what he [or she] does first."

When we are holding back to see what someone else is going to bring forward, we will never be able to create an authentic relationship. As long as we hold back, we will always attract people into our lives who hold back. My clients would say to me, "Well, Temple, I do not want to get hurt." So I would tell them, "That's right, you would rather hurt yourself by not being you."

When you are not you, you hurt yourself and you die a little. If you hold back and do not give of yourself because you're trying to save your heart, then that's the type of man or woman you will always attract—people who do not put their whole selves in and who do not come from the heart. They will never see you and love you from an open heart because you are choosing people who are holding back the same way you are. We are here to be ourselves and put our whole selves in. If you are truly you, then you will let people be and stay in your life; you won't allow them to "let" you not be yourself. Here's the true formula to seeing whether a person is meant to be your life love: Put him or her in a room with children and pets. If the children and the pets like the person, you are good to go. If they do not, *run!*

People often hold back from pursuing their dreams because some-where along the way they have been disappointed or rejected. When you stop pursuing your dreams and who you are meant to be, you are dying a little. When you stop pursuing your dreams, can you not see that you are disappointing and rejecting yourself?

Think about the song "Hallelujah" by Leonard Cohen, artists such as the Beatles, or the book series *Chicken Soup for the Soul*, which later became a must-have for enlightenment. These are three examples of how early rejection or an initial lack of success did not stop people from pursuing their dreams but rather prompted them to put their whole selves in.

It is essential that we put our whole selves in.

In life, we always get what we bring. So the question ("quest I on") becomes: What am I bringing to the experience?

I have also known a number of people who will spare themselves from getting another pet or another spouse because they can't bear losing them and going through the pain of loss again. These people are not putting their whole selves in; I have never met a person with this philosophy who isn't old long before his or her time. Remember, aging is natural, whereas being old is not. We are all created on the physical plane to age, yet being old is a frame of mind and not a spiritual truth. Individuals who are awake and love life are ageless spirits. Love is an energy that cannot be stored or not shared because of what may or may not happen. As Bob Dylan said, "He not busy being born is busy dying."

In the magical words of the "The Hokey Pokey," you put yourself in and you turn yourself around, but this doesn't mean that you have to turn yourself around first. The song does not tell you to "do the Hokey Pokey" *after* you turn yourself around" or to "turn yourself around and *then* do the Hokey Pokey." Most people delay the good in their lives, waiting until something is fixed, mended, or corrected, and only then will they put their whole selves in. From experience I can tell you that it rarely happens that way. Life is about putting your whole self in—*now*!

The irony is that, if most of us waited until we were living our own definition of perfection, we would never do anything. And that's where a lot of people are: dying every day while they wait to become *something* they are unwilling to attempt to step into. We would never put our whole selves in if we waited for everything to be in place before taking the first steps.

I would never have become a teacher and a leader if I had waited until I was free from working on something because as long as we are in human form, we are going to be working on something. The key to individuality is not being free from working on something; it is how the *something* is working through you.

A couple of years ago, my spiritual community hosted a creative art summer program for kids, and you could see their openness and their willingness to do it all. Whether it was African drumming, collage or watercolor, or tae kwon do or dancing, the kids did it all without hesitation because the whole intention of the program was to develop within them a freedom of self-expression; the allowance of that freedom of self-expression results in an increased self-esteem. Our intention throughout the program was connection, not perfection. Our intention from the beginning was to see each child from his or her wholeness. When we are little, we explore so many different things. We take a hairbrush, make it a microphone, and sing a song; we act out a character. We do not analyze all the made-up "what ifs" in the moment. We simply stay awake. We put our whole selves in.

We'll write down a poem we wrote, draw something or we'll make something out of little to no materials, and somewhere along the way we get into this inner critic, and, from either our own doing or someone else's, we begin the need to grade and judge ourselves or to say that we don't measure up. We start to focus on what we perceive or what we have been told is missing. We start wanting to measure the way in which we creatively express, believing that it has to be the best of the best for it to matter. Yet the only thing that really matters is to give our best intention to fully self-express. In order to fully self-express, we must put our whole selves in.

The Desire to Be Perfect

What causes the desire to be perfect? Through early programming, we look for approval outside ourselves rather than inwardly satisfying our own creative abilities. It's a repetitive cycle.

It's hard to see others as whole when we cannot or will not do what we need to do to see ourselves this way. We hold ourselves as less than perfect.

Big people want to make little people be like them, or be like they wish they could have been growing up. Often unconsciously, parents and guardians force their children to fulfill the unrealized covenants of their own sacred stories. The energy of the children is rarely allowed, and therefore from the very beginning they get the message that it is not safe to be themselves. Bullying has become the new concern in our society, but the truth, if only we will tell it, is that we received more bullying from our teachers, family members, and doctors than we did from our own peers. Generations of adults have stopped telling the truth about reality, so we are seeing more and more bullying because truth will always find its way to us, whether in the courage to express itself or in rage.

Parents also reward "right action" from a child by saying, "This makes mommy (daddy) proud." A child will clean up his toys or the little girl will make her bed, awaiting outside approval in the words "You make me proud." The real way to teach a child self-esteem and inner connection is to say to your child or grandchild when they do good deeds, "This must make you feel good about you."

Another challenge is that we rush children's lives to adulthood so they can be adults for 90 percent of their lives. Because we rush the process, we are not able to let children develop naturally so they can put their whole selves in. It is ridiculous to start telling a child at four and five to "be a big boy" or "be a big girl."

What are we really saying? Be a big person like me, so you can pay bills, have a mortgage, and be responsible for the rest of your life?

Children who do not get to be children, who are forced into early adulthood, and who are rushed into growing up rarely ever grow up. They die a little, and their inner anguish usually shows up in rage, bullying, or addiction.

You cannot rush a tree into growing tall; you will destroy it first.

My sixth-grade teacher told my parents that I was never going to amount to anything because I talked too much. If she had been interested in connection rather than perfection, she could have seen my heart through my eyes. She could have seen that I was hurting and needed to be validated and supported. Perhaps she could have realized that I had been fed sugar in the morning before I arrived at school and was hyped-up beyond my capacity to settle into the day. Perhaps she could have recognized that all that chatter occurred because no one was truly hearing me.

Intuitively she saw that I had the gift of talking, which I have been doing successfully all my life, but because she was not connected, she saw my gifts as negative. Her perfectionism caused me to doubt myself for many years and to die a little.

Most teachers, I hope, are not like that teacher. Nevertheless, we are still in an educational environment today that dictates doing things perfectly, that teaches us to specialize in certain areas rather than having a wide range of development. Taking art and music out of our school system hasn't helped this issue; it's a tremendous challenge now.

We are now putting such an emphasis on developing the intellectual aspects of our kids rather than creating a space for them to discover their innate and sacred gifts.

We are all created from a place of wholeness, but if we are always treated as broken and are driven to be perfect, we will not be able to fully self-express. We will rely instead on being nurtured, sometimes becoming needy because we long to heal ourselves. Rather than being childlike, which is essential for the creative spirit, we grow up by not growing up and remain childish instead. The wounded perfectionist is often the most needy. A whole person relies on the Creator, whereas a wounded person relies on circumstances and other people.

How can we change our reliance on outward circumstances and become more self-reliant? First we must decide that we are ready and willing to change. We often get to this point by realizing that our current way isn't working, or the inner ache to become more breaks us up so that we shift into more.

We must then accept that our parents, grandparents, and guardians did the best they had with what they knew and felt at the time. To hold on to the energy of resenting what our parents, grandparents, and guardians did not do for us allows this energy to be "re-sent" (reexpressed) over and over again until we let it go. Not only do we express this re-sent (resentment) energy to the world, we resend it to ourselves. In other words, we become the re-sentment and repetitive patterns that did not work for us in the first place. The very people we resent for their inability to properly raise us have created a long-term energy of stopping us from ever being raised. We must raise ourselves above our earthly stories and move into our sacred stories.

Since life does not go backward, we wake up and get in touch with the possibilities of how we can begin to honor who we really are right now. We pull out the list in our shielded and protected heart and allow the memories to resurface of the individuals we longed to be when we used to play on the playground. In other words, we have our own christening ceremony and call forth the true dreams and ideals we once longed for, and in some small or significant way we begin to apply these longings—we put our whole selves in. We hold on to the feelings of what it will be like when we become the energy we are dreaming of. Once this declaration is in motion, life begins to change. New energies of possibilities appear. The heart begins to open and feel. We begin to heal through what we turn toward, not what we have been turning away from.

Once awakened, we never return to this place of perfectionism again, nor do we impose it on other children. We wake up, and over time we become childlike again. We model to the children the open heart. It won't happen overnight, any more than we became this way overnight. Yet overnight we will develop a new template for who we really are. By the time I was thirteen, I had written and placed upon my wall this statement: *Today I found me. I do not like what I see. I don't expect you to. But I must be me in order to become what I am supposed to be.*

One of the main reasons I continued to sabotage my greatness over and over in my life is that I did not want to be found out. I did not want people to see me, for at that time in the rural South, you feared for your life if you did not conform, and I had been abandoned so many times by the few people I had trusted to really see me and love me. If your parents can't love you as you are, it is hard to conceptualize that there is a God out there somewhere who loves you, whom you don't even know and who doesn't seem to know you. Otherwise, why would you have been born to people who do not know you or understand enough to know you?

I am grateful that at an early age I found God in nature, in music, and in the arts. Because of drawing and music and playing in a band, I was able to develop a stronger sense of self-esteem. My years as a successful athlete made me want to stay on Earth rather than leave it. Many experiences I learned as an athlete and in art and music classes created the competence and the confidence that I draw on to this day.

One reason we aren't teaching most children to put their whole selves in is that we no longer expose them to nature to experience things like a vision quest and nature exploring. We are not providing children with the opportunity to connect with nature so that they will understand their inner connection to their Creator and all living things. Time spent in natural settings, outdoors, and in the country supports children in developing their imaginations and an inner sense of mystery. We are now raising children who stay indoors and spend most of their time on machines and with technology. We are more connected than ever to anything, everyone, and anything else, yet we are less connected to ourselves.

Is staying indoors on a machine a pattern in your own day-to-day existence? Begin now to make outdoor experiences a priority in your life rather than just a necessity for getting from one place to another. Take time to visit parks, beaches, go bicycling and do outdoor activities with your friends and family. Create space on a weekly basis for sitting in nature and connecting with the earth. For many years, my shaman teacher would have me take my shoes off and, with my bare feet on the earth, visualize pulling the energy from the earth into my body. This exercise was very effective in keeping me balanced and grounded.

For those of you who live in freezing weather for months that prevents you from being outside on a regular basis, plan during these times to visit natural history museums, watch wildlife documentaries, and find other ways to enhance your connection to nature.

We are dying a little every day, and we are not putting our whole selves in. It is my intention, through sacred storytelling in each of these chapters, that you will have several "aha" moments and awakenings so that you may put your whole selves in and learn how to turn yourselves around.

My Family of Origin Versus My Creation Story

I grew up in a small town surrounded by a group of people who were loving yet small-minded. I remember observing them when I was a little girl, watching how they interacted with one another, how they made decisions about their lives, and the reasons behind their habits and beliefs. I was really little the first time I asked why we believed a certain way, and I continued to ask this same question for many years. The answer was always the same: "That's just the way it is." This was my first inkling of why people begin to die: they never have the chance to fully live by asking questions that create originality.

We are not robotic in nature. We are born surrounded by water, and our bodies consist of 90 percent water, so we are made to be open to the fluidity and flexibility of our unfoldment. To be born is one of the most amazing miracles of all time. To be born many times within a lifetime allows us to witness how the miracle of our original birth can become realized time and again. When individuals are born as these amazing and original creative spirits, they will begin to die from the moment they are not allowed the freedom to be and express as they are destined to do.

I questioned my grandmother Lois on many occasions about why we were Baptists and why we seemed hypocritical, and her answer was always "Temple, this is the way it is. Now stop asking and have faith." This was so confusing to me, for I did have faith. I had great faith in the presence of God, a higher power who spoke to me every

User name: HELLE, AMANDA
J.

Title: Victim of grace : when
God's goodness prevails
Author: Gunn, Robin Jones,
1955-
Item ID: R2001926118
Date due: 1/4/2018,23:59
Current time: 12/07/2017,
17:52

Title: Miracles from Heaven :
a little girl, her journey
Author: Beam, Christy.
Item ID: R2003758162
Date due: 1/4/2018,23:5
Current time: 12/07/201/
17:52

Title: When did you die? : 8
steps to stop dying every d
Author: Hayes, Temple.
Item ID: R2002514061
Date due: 1/4/2018,23:59
Current time: 12/07/2017,
17:53

Title: Four cups : God's
timeless promises for a li
of
Author: Hodges, Chris.
Item ID: R2001910716
Date due: 1/4/2018,23:59
Current time: 12/07/2017,
17:53

day. Where was everyone else who was unique? And why did the idea of uniqueness seem so foreign to everyone around me? What was the point, anyway?

How did I get to be in a family where no one saw me or understood me? I thought I must have been adopted.

Our beliefs as Baptists were so hypocritical. When John was sick, we would say, "Oh, God is working on him." Yet when Mary was ill, people at the church would say, "Oh, the devil has hold of her." I remember thinking, *How does a human get to decide this? We are not seeing who God is; we are seeing who we are*—a very limited perspective. And even though I did not have the words for it then as I do now, I knew it was wrong and that we were dying a little.

I really understood what hypocrisy was when I was with my nanny and other African American people throughout my childhood. They were as important to me as anyone else, but my grandmother Lois forbade me to go to the wedding of one of my dearest friends. She said I could not go because what would people think of me? I was sixteen years old, and I would be the only white girl there. I did not understand what had suddenly happened to our principles of love and caring for one another. Where was our faith at the time my friend needed me to use it by living it? What were we saying, that we could care about them privately but not publicly?

Well, guess what. I went to that wedding!

We talked about the death of Jesus from a place of fear, yet we rarely celebrated His life from a place of joy. Somehow we had missed His entire sacred creation story, for we only seemed to worship that He died and missed out on the entire message of how He lived. His message was inclusiveness, being nonjudgmental and showing how we are connected to our Creator. I did not understand the incongruency of the message. If Jesus hung out with the Samaritan woman, why could I not go to my dear friend's wedding? Who were we, anyway?

When I was a kid, my friends always said I was way too deep and heavy. I somehow knew better about a lot of things yet did not know why. I had the ability to read energies and know when people were being false to themselves. I would hear my classmates make up stories for the teacher, such as "I'm sorry, I didn't do my homework because my dad has been real sick." Somehow I knew that to lie was to die, but how did I know this? I seemed to innately know that when you know better but do not do better, there is a price to pay. The price is the inability to have an authentic, empowered, and energetic life. The price is that you die a little. You cannot have anything real if you are unable to express anything real. You can get in life only what you bring.

I was twenty years old when a friend invited me to Unity Church in Greenville, South Carolina. For the first time in my life, I heard someone say, "You are God's beloved child with whom God is well pleased." I cried all day and all night after hearing that. I decided that day to stop dying, at least in the way I had been mentally treating myself. Someone actually found me lovable: God loved me. I knew this, but no one had ever said it to me. I had lived my whole life trying to prove that God did not make a mistake when I was created, and I would live long enough to understand that there is a big difference between making a mistake and being one. When all the people who surround you have an outdated, constricted version of God, you start to deny your natural intuition after a while.

I am so grateful to Don Bliss for thinking enough of me to introduce me to a place that practiced a true connection to God. This was the start of true bliss for me and was a key factor in my being found. Knowing that I was God's beloved with whom God was well pleased stopped the cycle I was living every day of wanting to die rather than live. I know had I not found this way of living, I would not have found a way to live.

Twenty years of waiting to be validated and recognized is a very long time.

Once the doors of the heart begin to open, they can never truly be closed again. The energy of change brings significant avenues into your life. Once I had been awakened to the inner truth that I was God's beloved, most things in my life changed. I moved to a new area, got involved in group therapy, and became sober all within a few years. When the inner, natural shift occurs, there is no returning to a shielded heart and a straitjacket.

My First Experience with Soul Retrieval

Several years ago, I went to visit a woman who had lost her husband very unexpectedly at forty-two years old. I was in awe when I saw that she had so much energy in her body. Most people I had witnessed in my life who had experienced the physical death of a loved one would have a grayish color about them, yet she was so vibrant and light. She told me about a visit she had had with a shaman who had done soul retrieval on her by leading her through a deep meditation and retrieving aspects of her life when she was fragmented, weary, and losing her vibrancy; this process helped her retrieve her energy. I was amazed. In just the way life works, I thought I was being there for her when in reality she was being there for me. I thought I was spending my time giving to her when in truth she was giving to me. I was waking up.

I did not call the shaman she had consulted, nor did I immediately purchase the book she suggested: *Soul Retrieval* by Sandra Ingerman. If you had known me then, you would realize that this hesitation was in itself a modern-day miracle. Up to this point I had lived my life by the paradigm that something was missing, so when the woman told me about something I did not have, the me of the past would have wanted it right away. In retrospect, I realize I was starting to awaken to my natural self, not pushing a new direction in my life but allowing it to unfold. This was a way of being that I had forgotten up until then. This was the beginning of being reborn into the me I was born to be: the healer and the listener of knowing when to do and knowing when to be.

I prayed to my Creator that, if my soul needed to be retrieved, to provide me with the means and way in which this could be possible. I called this experience into my being. I prayed it into my existence. I also eventually bought *Soul Retrieval* and absolutely could not put it down once I started to read it. It was bringing me back to life. I had a new map, a new road on which I felt the light was shining again to bring me back home to finding me.

I was leading a weekly group called the Foundation for Great People, and, one week when I had to be absent, I asked my friend and assistant, Mitzi, to book a teacher in my place. When I returned from my vacation, I asked Mitzi how it went. She said, "Oh, it was amazing. This shaman came and talked to us about soul retrieval."

In that moment, I knew! I got the shaman's number and called her to request a visit. On my drive over to Berenice Andrews's home, I received an intuitive message that she was to be my teacher, she at the same time received an intuitive message that I was to be her student, and my life began again. I was beginning to be born. I was beginning to wake up.

My retrieval experience revealed to me the major moments of my life when I was little and was beginning to die.

When I was five years old, I ate mothballs and had my stomach pumped. I thought it was sugar for the horse.

At seven, I saw my grandfather Howard, whom I adored, being driven up to his driveway and dumped in his yard, dead drunk and passed out.

At ten years old, I was picked up by my grandfather Johnny Temple Hayes to go to church one fine Sunday morning. I was so excited to spend time with him but also anxious. He was always angry when my parents weren't going to church, and he did not like having to come and get me. When we were driving away, I looked back, and my dog was following us. I shared with my grandfather that I had to get him back to the house. Oh, boy, did he become furious.

As I ran the dog back down the road, my grandfather drove in reverse to meet me, and he accidentally hit me and knocked me in the ditch. He made me clean up, and we went to church as though nothing had happened. He did not have the wisdom to understand that he could have given me a spiritual lesson right there on the side of the road. Church is more than attendance in a building; it is a way of life. Many people in all parts of the country do not seem to have that inner wisdom, and therefore the people around them die a little. Church is more than a place you go to; it is the inner wisdom from which you live. A true church will teach you to live by the principles it represents wherever you are.

When I was almost eleven, my mother was taken from me briefly and severely punished, ridiculed, and ousted from the family for allegedly having an affair. She was given shock treatments, and she was not able to remember much about my childhood, her childhood, or anything else. My childhood ended that week, for I realized that adults who were told what to do did not always know what they were doing. They destroyed the vibrancy of my mother; thus they destroyed my vibrant trust of people, which until then had been innate in me.

The love that saved me was the deep, unconditional love I felt from my pets. But then my dad stepped on my kitten and killed it. He cursed me and it and threw it in the trash. He also ran over my favorite dog with his truck as I was standing there right beside the dog. My dad had to get where he was going; he was always in a hurry—the place he was could never be enough. So he slung the dog's body into the back of the truck. That day he also slung my heart in there with my dog-friend, and it would take me years to recover from my resentment of how he killed everything I loved—including me, in my early years. When I was eleven, I was sitting in the backseat of a car and leaning forward when the driver slammed on the brakes. I flew with the movement of the seat and chipped my front tooth on the dashboard. My tooth was broken in half, and on the broken edge there was black paint from the car. My father would not let me get it fixed, so I went around with a broken tooth for a few years. For a child, this felt like an eternity. I always held back a full smile. This certainly lasted long enough for me to die a little, and lots of kids made fun of me. The irony was that my childhood had literally taken away my smile. My smile of life was dying.

When I was thirteen, my parents discovered that I was having a sexual relationship with a seventeen-year-old girl and forbade me to ever see her again. My father took me to a health clinic, and I feared they would do to my mind and brain what they had done to my mother's. I lied to survive. My lie made me die a little, and I lived this lie for another thirty years. I lost my true love, and therefore I lost the joy of true love in me.

As deep-rooted Southern Baptists, my family was shamed by me, and my grandmother Lois told me she was sorry that she was not going to see me in heaven. I was thirteen years old when she said this to me. She was disappointed in me both sexually and spiritually. The God of her understanding led her to the belief that I had two tickets to hell. I died a lot that day because I had believed in her. I also thought she believed in me.

When I was fourteen, my favorite cousin, Bruce Vermillion, was tragically killed in a car accident. He was one of the rare people who could see me for me. He was driving with friends to celebrate his decision to become a minister, and a woman ran a red light and killed him.

After my cousin died, I knew I didn't want to die a physical death. I was getting this idea in my head that if you are good you will die young. As a Baptist there was Jesus and in my family there was Bruce. I was already emotionally dead, but I wasn't ready to leave my life, so when I was fourteen, I started drinking and smoking heavily. The first time I drank I became very ill, but I continued. The first time I smoked I got tonsillitis. I refused to listen to the signs and my own intuition, so I did not flow with what was natural and therefore died a little.

At seventeen, my grandfather Johnny Temple Hayes died—the man who gave me his name, Temple. The man who had given me such a special name never understood that I was truly special, and he died before he could live enough to see the truth—not only of his own nature but also of mine.

All these events created the subtle deaths in my life and had never been addressed. I had been in therapy and group therapy through-out the years and had done lots of storytelling at bars, but never had anyone addressed the parts of myself that were dying.

I never consciously wanted to die, yet unconsciously I—at least, the "me" that no one seemed to be comfortable with—did not trust enough to want to live. As those missing energetic pieces were retrieved over time, I started to wake up and be reborn. I started finding me for the first time in many years. I started feeling at home. I started to feel that my world was changing.

When I first started working with shamanism, my teacher, Berenice Andrews, gave me the assignment of writing down every major event that had occurred in my life (both kind and unkind). I had a very organized story of all the times I had been hurt by my family or wounded by someone else's invasion (some of the events already listed in this chapter). My list included the old man at the park who became my "friend," only to later attempt to attack me physically and sexually when I was eleven. Where was God in those moments?

This old man had worked me at every angle—for instance, telling me he knew my grandfather Johnny. He said very nice things to me as he prepared one week to seduce me. Where was the love of God in those moments of my life?

It was one of the most amazing exercises because as I started to list each and every event in chronological order, I began to see how everything had been perfectly orchestrated, time and again, to develop me on my path. I began to see that each time I was wounded, when I declared that God was busy and unavailable, the Universe had actually been working overtime to protect and connect me with my path. I was the one who was shielded and part of the walking dead, who was unavailable—God had nothing to do with it.

This is key to putting your whole self in.

Cut some sheets of paper into small pieces (about three square inches each), and on each piece write down an event in your life when you felt disconnected, saddened, or compromised in any way. Do not get into analyzing the moments that took your energy away; simply write the headlines of the moments down. List each event on a separate piece of paper. Do not spare yourself from anything you can possibly remember.

When you finish writing down all the events, go through them all, and rather than seeing them and feeling them as something that happened to you, look at them in terms of how they shaped you. See in the events how they created within you wisdom, insight, courage, and tenacity. Begin to bless the events, and rather than holding on to them for how they hurt or damaged you, see ultimately how they have defined and shaped you.

I used to tell my students of spirituality that if each of them threw all their life problems on the floor, each of them would run to get their own back. Our sacred stories can be written and lived only by defining and redefining these moments in our lives.

The purpose of my life was not to continue to die a little. My life purpose was to learn with my new sacred creation story how I could truly live. There were moments that were fun to experience, and there were moments that broke my heart so that my heart would open to the new me of my inner understanding.

Once I began to see how necessary all these kind and unkind events had been in my life, I could never go back to seeing my life and being with it in the same way. I started seeing moments in my life as necessary to continue to shape my sacred story.

I started following life like the "connect the dots" coloring books we played with when we were children. Through this new practice, I made my most significant discovery: life had never been against me but had always been for me.

All the tragedies, all the tears, all the denials and addictions, all the times someone either did not like me or see me or understand who I was, all the days that I felt spit on, all the shame I carried in my heart until I could come out at forty-five years old (once I had told my mother), all the moments I drank and almost killed myself in a car, the two times I was in jail for driving a vehicle while under a great unnatural influence, all the days and ways I had died a little and didn't want to be here—all of these moments were connecting my dots so I could live to be on the other side with a depth that a CD, a book, or simple training could not have given me. I understood that the tragedies of my life no longer had to describe me. These events had been created to define me so I could put my whole self in.

There is nothing to lose and everything to gain. These events had occurred so my world could truly change.

This is how I found me and the art of coming home. I am humbled that you are spending this time of your life with me on my journey, and although I share many stories about my family and my original religion, please know that my intention is never to blame; it is simply to claim. My life was always instructive, though at times painful, and I lived long enough to realize that my family members could never have loved me any more than they loved themselves. Their definition of love was simply not enough to fit in my definition. Because of their lack of love, I had to discover true inner love.

I had to claim the Creator of my existence, who thought enough of me to create me so I may continue to be created. The same Creator is working within you as well to create your own unique story of birth and rebirth. Traditionally, Christians are taught that we must experience salvation to truly live, but the true spiritual teaching is that we must be saved from ourselves to live a full and prosperous life. We must save and retrieve the parts of ourselves that we have allowed to die while we are living.

All the Pieces Are in Your Box

When I was little, one of the many moments I cherished was putting together a puzzle with my grandmother Rubye. Doing a jigsaw puzzle was always fun, especially when we would get near to completion. There would always be one or two pieces that we could not find or that did not seem to fit. We would keep going back to the image on the box and see a color or something on the image that would make us feel confident that the piece would be discovered soon. Never did it occur to us to question the manufacturer about whether the piece was actually there. At times we would almost want to force-fit certain pieces just so we could be done with the puzzle.

Our lives are like a jigsaw puzzle. We trust the manufacturer to provide us with every piece of the puzzle to give us what we need to obtain the image on the box, yet often we do not believe in the manufacturer (our Creator) of our lives. We have all the pieces we need to be the amazing and incredible image we were destined to be. When we force-fit the pieces, we are not able to allow the proper process of our journey to occur. We cannot put our whole selves in.

In all my years of counseling, I can easily say, all the people (including me) who have forced events in their lives would do anything to take those moments back. A force-fit life adventure never works out for an individual who chooses to live with energy, vibrancy, and youthfulness. It is going against the grain, like the way it hurts when we rub our hand in the wrong direction against a grain of wood. We can get to the other side of the wood, but not without a lot of splinters.

When we live by the premise of wounds and the belief that our puzzle does not have all the pieces, we are not wearing the right set of glasses to see the good in our lives.

A Vow to Our Creator

We have all, by the very nature of our birth, made a vow to our Creator. And equally and simultaneously, our Creator has made a vow to us and a covenant with us. We are here to express the divine image in which we have been created. When we deny our natural path by not listening to our *God-Personalized System*—our *GPS*—we find a life of increased pain and sorrow. Until we allow the authentic nature of our being to shine through, we will be dying in our everyday existence. We have accepted that outside situations and circumstances have power over our lives and dictate what we are to believe and how we are to be.

A few years ago I was meeting one of my friends at a restaurant in Florida, and across the table, in the center aisle, a little girl was performing and speaking as if she had an audience of hundreds. I said hello to her and asked where she was from. She said, "I am from South

Carolina," and I said, "So am I." Then she started performing, doing a somersault right in the middle of the restaurant, and she declared, "I am seven"—as if to say, I am ready to live life fully. I am so excited about my life. I am so excited about living—*yipppeee!*

Being excited about life is being thankful you were given life, while being excited about living is how you allow yourself to experience the moments of your life.

I was so touched by this young girl's presence and was reminded of myself at an early age and the value of remaining as free as she appeared to be. She was doing her best to be as close to her divine nature as possible. She triggered within me how I was losing this ability and had died a little. Of course, her grandfather was in the background telling me how much trouble she was and that he wished she would sit down and behave. She was a difficult child, he said, because she wanted to do things her way. Imagine! I have wondered about her many times, how long it was before she began to die to who she truly was.

One day, the story is told, when Buddha was gathered with many of his followers, they kept asking him, "How did you do it? What did you do? How did it happen that you could be enlightened?" They were all ready to hear the amazing news. And Buddha simply said, "I am awake. I am awake."

We must wake up. We must be born to who we truly are. It's time to move from being disconnected and drained to feeling impassioned and energized about our lives.

If you aren't excited about your life, don't expect anyone else to be.

It's time to wake up!

Ideas to Process and Integrate

~~≈≈⚬⚬⚬≈≈~~

The key to individuality is not being free from working on something; it is how the something is working through you.
When you are not you, you hurt you and you die a little.

Take the time to write in your journal all the areas and moments of your life in which you are not truly being you. (This does not mean you will be required to leave these areas in order to be you, but writing it down will help you see how you continue to leave yourself.)

What areas of your life are you not putting your whole self in? How would your life be different if you did?

Aim for connection rather than perfection.

Begin today to observe, in your interactions with yourself and others, when you are into connection and when you are coming from perfection. This new way of looking at and expressing your ways of being will totally transform you.

We are all created from a place of wholeness, but, if we are always treated as broken and driven to be perfect, we will not be able to fully self-express.

Begin the new practice of connecting in a deeper way to nature and seeing the nature of all of the events as part of your sacred story. Then you will begin to notice an inner power that did not exist before. You will begin to see yourself in a new light and lighten up with your life.

I understand that the tragedies of my life are no longer necessary to describe me. I can embrace these events instead as necessary to shape and define me.

Make a list of all the times in your childhood, as I did, when you felt wounded, disconnected, and discounted. Embrace these moments that started you on the path of sleeping at the wheel and dying a little. Once you go through the process of seeing these events as defining and shaping you rather than being tragic and unnecessary, you will begin to notice new life in your body. You will start to feel awake and more alive. You will begin to feel more at home.

If you aren't excited about your life, don't expect anyone else to be.

2

From Fear to Feeling to Freedom

Step Two: How to Walk into Your Life by Walking Through Your Life

United we stand; divided we are merely a distraction. Not only is this true with the world, it is also true for us as individuals. If we divide ourselves between the feelings we approve of and the ones we disapprove of, we will have a life filled with distractions rather than purpose.

I was born an eagle but realized over time that eagles did not exist in my part of the woods.

I had to let the ways of being an eagle fade, for to be an eagle meant I would stand out above the rest, and to stand out above the rest meant my life would be taken from me.

I saw another group of birds that had wings as I did, but they never left the ground. They were chickens. They did not seem to think about flying, and they did everything the farmer said, so I watched how they lived. They were afraid to fly even though they had wings. They were afraid to run even though they had all the physical parts I had. They simply seemed to settle on being chickens. I played like them, ate like them, and made noises like them, but deep inside I knew I was different from them. The fence never stopped my longing to be free, and pretending never made it so. It was fear that stopped me from being an eagle.

One day the fence was open just enough, and I found my way out. I flew like an eagle once again. It wasn't hard to fly. Actually, it was harder to be a chicken than it was to fly like an eagle.

Feeling the Fear

Perhaps you felt fear and did the thing you feared anyway, but the fear came back. If this is the case, then most likely the fear wasn't truly felt; it was simply processed through thinking it away rather than feeling it away. Fear will return time and again until the individual goes deep inside and does not hold back. It's like painting with new paint on top of preexisting paint that is cracking on the wall. You can paint on top of it, but it will not last. New paint will last only if you invest the time it takes to scrape away the old and then apply the new.

A lot of the work many of us did initially when we were feeling our fears involved different acronyms. My initial introduction to dealing with fear was by using the acronym FEAR: *False Evidence Appearing Real.*

And then I created my own meaning. I had done some deep work on how I had projected reasons to be afraid onto my experiences, but what really held me back was being afraid that I would repeat a situation again. So now the acronym FEAR had a new meaning: *Former Experiences Actually Repeating.*

This showed up as being afraid, as I stood at the front of a room ready to speak, that I would forget what I was going to say. I was afraid that people would freeze as I froze when I could not remember my point or where I was going.

I was also afraid of being found out—that because of such rejection from my family and from my religion as a child, I would lose people I loved if they really knew me. I could only go so far with a relationship, because if I got too close and shared too much about my life, both spiritually and sexually, I would lose the person's affection. No matter what I told myself as an adult or how much I improved my confidence, my talents, or my self-esteem, the inner child within me would shiver at the thought of being rejected or abandoned again.

I was not putting my whole self in because I was afraid to. This is really crucial to living a life that is impassioned and energized. It is so important to see the various responses we have to situations and really feel them so we can be free of them. This deep inner work is so necessary to our sacred creation story. We will continue to die a little every day until we move from fear to honoring our feelings to freedom.

If we deal with our fears and feelings at a surface level, then we will have experiences at a surface level. If we feel the fears at a surface level and do the next step anyway, then the next step will carry us to the next place, yet with very little depth.

As long as we are afraid of expressing our full selves, we will die a little while we are living. As long as we are afraid, we will never trust the life that has been created for us. As long as we are afraid, we will not trust our Creator and have the amazing benefits that come naturally from a free-flowing God-ordained life. The covenant God has offered to us is there for the taking, yet the acceptance of the covenant is entirely our choice. We have been given free will to choose whether we accept heaven on Earth.

Where does this deep-rooted fear come from? From my own experiences, I would have to say that some of us brought it into this lifetime with us. (Many of us have realized by now that this lifetime is not our only incarnation.) From the time I can remember my own observations of life, I had an immense fear that something terrible was going to happen to me.

I was probably six years old when I first started showing signs of this phobia. I washed my hands all the time. If I went outside and touched the tire on the car or moved a can in the carport or helped someone else move a can or a bucket, I would hold my hands up until I could clean them. I would often convince myself that there could be some type of poison on whatever I had touched and that it would hurt me.

I was always afraid something would happen to me. I had a tremendous fear of letting my guard down around people who said they loved me. My grandfather had hit me with his car, my father had killed my pets, I was afraid I would be forced to have shock therapy, and my mother had changed because of bad decisions made by others, so I was always awaiting the next events that could possibly happen to me.

However, rather than feeling the feelings of being afraid and deeply wounded, I simply went on to the next moment, guarded yet participatory. These weren't conscious and constant fears, yet they would reveal themselves from time to time and take my breath away. I began to separate and hold myself back from people, places, and experiences because of the fear of what could happen next. I did not have panic attacks, but I did shut down. I clenched my jaw for so many years that I had to have major jaw surgery when I was 29 years old. I was imprisoned time and again by my inability to speak the truth of who I really was, both spiritually and sexually. I ground my teeth all the way down in the back, and my jaw no longer functioned properly.

One day, in my late thirties, I was driving across the state of Florida, enjoying the scenery, the landscape, and the immense blessings of nature, when all of a sudden I had a strong thought: *What if I swallowed my tongue on this long country road and died? How long would it take someone to find me?* This was before we all had cell phones.

With this fleeting fear—which took me almost out of my body, because I could barely breathe—I realized that I needed to share this with someone, so I told my shaman teacher and confidant during our next appointment.

As I mentioned earlier, I was raised in the South, where you do not share your deep secrets. I had learned to tell my teachers and the other people in my life only the good things they wanted to hear, so for me to tell my teacher—who had been telling me how gifted I was as a healer—that I had such deep fears was a huge breakthrough. I was so afraid that I would diminish in her eyes and that she would be disappointed in me.

This fear, like a constantly open window running on my computer, had been an integral part of my life long enough, and I was ready to do something about it. I began to list all the things I had been afraid of over the years, and although I had outgrown some of them, like the need to always wash my hands, new fears would take their place. As a kid, I saw someone trying to get in my window; as an adult I felt dark energy outside the door. And now I was telling Berenice Andrews, my shaman teacher, that for no reason whatsoever I feared swallowing my tongue and dying on the highway.

It was an incredible relief to share all these things with another person and never feel judged for my words, my fears, and my feelings. Immediately, what I noticed the most was that just naming and claiming the fears gave me relief. I could now see clearly in my life there is no breakthrough without feeling the 'ache' (break) and 'ooh' (through). It is so common for us in our humanness to feel some of the ache and never approach the "walking through" part.

My Sacred Warrior Shield

I was told by my teacher to go into prayer and ask for a divine symbol that would resonate with me energetically. I was to use this symbol as a sacred warrior shield. Each time I had a deep fear or a thought of danger, I was to hold up this shield, and it would deflect and dissipate the energy.

I went into a deep meditation and asked what symbol I needed in order to face, change, and transcend my experiences with fear. The image appeared to me in a few seconds, and when I came back from the meditation I drew it on a piece of paper

What came to me was a symbol of the outer shell of a heart held by my hands at each side.

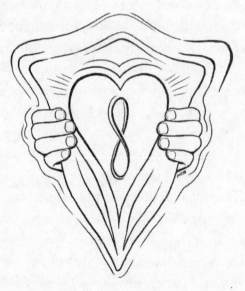

When I was alone, I would hold this shield up physically, as if I were holding a real shield in front of me. When I was with others, I would simply visualize it in my mind and bless the ritual. I knew I could get just as much effect from visualizing the action as from physically doing the action.

I was amazed, as I practiced this conscious intention, by how many times I actually had fear-based thoughts throughout the course of a day. It was almost overwhelming. I felt paranoid if someone did not speak to me a certain way or if I called someone and did not hear back from him or her. I was afraid of hearing from an event planner that I would not get to speak at a certain event after they had already committed to me. There was always a tape running in my head that I would get rejected or abandoned. I was afraid that I would not have enough money or that my dreams were never going to be realized. I was afraid of getting old long before I was ready to do so. I was afraid I would be left by someone somewhere. I was afraid that if people really knew I was afraid, they wouldn't love me.

My shadow self sought to get me to quit working with myself and to say it was silly. My shadow wanted me to stop this crazy exercise. My shadow wanted me to accept that it was too much work to change, when the truth is that it is too much work to be determined to keep things the same. I was on the cusp of being born again, and being born again so we will stop dying requires a few new stretch marks, to say the least.

I had almost become comfortable being a chicken even though deep down I always knew I was an eagle destined for an "eagle's life." The eagle within me continued to call me to keep going.

I was persistent, and, even though it was uncomfortable, I persevered. *Quitter* is not a common word in my vocabulary. For the first several days, it felt totally consuming. Yet I stayed with the process each and every time a fear came up. One day it occurred to me that

I had not had a particular fear for a few days. That realization freed me as I have never been freed before. The depth of fear that was once normal for me rarely happens to me now. When it occurs, I hold up my sacred warrior shield.

I also had to realize that I had been conditioned for so much of my life to not feel okay that even when I did feel okay, I would look for something to justify why I couldn't just feel okay and be happy. I felt out of place as a kid, and I created that same feeling as an alcoholic, always apologizing and thinking that I had done something wrong. Yet even though these things had long since changed, I was still carrying around the core belief that I am not okay. This was not something I could change through the intellect; it required me to discover it through my heart. Not being okay had felt so natural for so long that I felt lost without it. It was quite some time before being okay became natural. This is a process that many people stop way too soon. I know, for I was almost one of them. I almost missed being an eagle instead of a chicken.

When you look into your own life, you might see that you do not have a fear of danger. You might not have, as I did, a fear of abandonment or rejection. You might not have carried in your life for many years that you are not okay or that you are a mistake. For you it could just be a fear that you don't deserve good things, that you are not "enough," or that you might be found out. These worries stop us in our tracks on the unconscious level, and we will sabotage our progress until we clear them up.

If you are looking at your life and seeing repetitive patterns of fear-based living, then this process of facing it, feeling it, and walking through it will change your life. If you do not recognize any of these fears as paralyzing your life—which would surprise me, since this book found you—then you are still blessed, for our society is saturated with people whose lives are driven by their fears, and you will therefore have lots of opportunities to teach others the simple exercise of creating a personal sacred warrior shield. It has changed the lives of hundreds of people I have coached and mentored because ancient solutions work, and they are immediate.

The teachings of shamanic leaders—Jesus, Buddha, Krishna, Krishnamurti, Yogananda, and many others—are all extremely simple. Yet the dedication to apply them and practice them on a daily basis in their simplicity is often what stops us. We have the tendency to believe that healing from what binds us has to be complicated, but it does not. Since we believe it has to be complicated, however, it reveals itself to us as complicated. The complication is often that we do enough to get by, which makes us feel slightly better yet rarely frees us. When we are willing to stay the course and fully commit to being totally alive, impassioned, and energized, the layers we need to shed will peel away very quickly.

The sacred warrior shield allowed me the opportunity to free myself from a lot of head chatter and noise inside myself, which opened the door for new ways to reveal themselves. We continue to peel off the layers. We say that the truth will reveal itself at the time it is ready; not only is this a true statement, it is a true reality. As we own our feelings and clear our feelings, we are able to get to the deeper issues that created all the small inadequacies in the first place.

When you step into not dying every day and are committed to a truly impassioned and energized life, it is essential to move from fears to feelings to freedom. As you face the fears and address the feelings that go with them, you will no longer have the feelings of being drained and disconnected, for you will no longer be disconnected from yourself and drained from being something you are not.

I had to recognize the fear and own it, feel it, and allow a solution to emerge so I could have freedom. My life soared after this experience. New experiences that in the past would have paralyzed me with fear came into my life. Platforms in front of large audiences emerged, and travel opportunities came from many different places. Before, I would have found reasons and excuses not to move forward, and even though I seemed so secure and powerful on the outside, my inner being had been saying something else. The old me could no longer stop the new, emerging me.

Take the time in your life to truly address each and every fear. Where fear exists, the heart will remain closed. Where fear exists, we will always be chickens rather than eagles.

Until we clear the inner fears, we will always respond to news and information from a place of reactiveness rather than a balanced perspective. Until we clear the fears, we will always be people who live their entire lives with other people telling them what to do.

The Old Rugged Cross Fear

One of the most common unconsciously driven fears that many people in our culture have, and are perhaps totally unaware of, comes from the bombardment of traditional Christian teaching. This teaching is portrayed over and over again, and it is in our psyches. Whether you are a nonbeliever—if that is even possible, for you are still a believer of what you do not believe—or you are Jewish, Hindu, Muslim, Buddhist, Wiccan, or any other religion, you are still not spared the image of Jesus being brutally killed and hanging on a cross. This image is everywhere.

The retail cross industry is bringing in billions of dollars—crosses with Jesus hanging on them and crosses that are empty. This is a fear-based and patriarchal way of looking at life that programs and trains all of us on a deep level to believe with fear that if you are a good person ordained by God, you will be killed. Don't get close to God because you could be murdered. If you draw attention to yourself because you can perform modern-day miracles, eventually people will hang you on the cross and leave you for dead. If you are a good person, you will be betrayed. If you are a good person, you will be abandoned.

When we believe this, we ultimately betray and abandon ourselves. We "hang" in our lives, somewhere between being good and being bad, in just a safe enough position so we will not die, while all the time we are dying from not truly living.

The irony in this is that as much as the deep-rooted evangelists shout and swear that Jesus died for you so you can get to a greater place, this approach actually *keeps* a person from stepping into his or her divinity and greater place. This is because at a core fundamental level within, the individual cannot overcome on the unconscious level that goodness comes with a price. A price of your life.

When we look at the preachers' kids and wonder why they are the biggest partyers of the gang, this should explain it. Some of the gifted and the geniuses in our culture are plagued with alcoholism and addiction, too. There is an underlying belief that bad people do not die young ("only the good die young") or that bad people can have a real good party on Earth and then, just before it's time to leave, they can "repent" and everything will be okay. How many times have you heard someone say, "She is a royal pain and will outlive all of us"? Why do we say this? On an unconscious level, we believe good people do not last. We believe masters will be hung on the cross. And we will do anything to sabotage our gifts and talents so we do not have to be one of them.

We have sacrificed the true message of Jesus that says know your connection to your true Father/Creator and you can have a life full of miracles. We have been taught a very misguided and misleading message that has caused us to live a miracle of being dead while we are alive. We have sacrificed a life that could be filled with magic and wonder and settled to create miracles of repeatedly doing the same old things over and over again. Let's face it—to repeatedly mess up your life time and time again is a miracle sadly working in reverse.

For centuries, many healers, great poets, and artists have died on the inside long before their time because of the "woundology" of the old rugged cross.

We use the phrase "I was scared to death" because we have felt this fear throughout the course of our lives, and we die a little each time this paradox is fed into our psyches. We cannot surrender to goodness, for we are inherently afraid that we will die, and when we deny that we will die, we deny our goodness. We have an inner saboteur to mess things up for us. We name it the "teenage years," an "immature" person, or "midlife crisis" and make it sound normal, yet the denial of one's goodness and the ability to do miracles will never be normal.

We are all birthed with the God-ordained intention to make miracles. Just the very fact that we are able to sabotage our lives and drive the consistent good from ourselves shows us that we can do miracles. The very fact that we can mess up our lives time and again is itself a modern-day miracle. Yet imagine using our ability to create miracles of greatness rather than miracles of lack, crisis, and limitation.

As long as we believe the cross is rugged, we will never outgrow the splinters that come with it. We will never learn to go with the "natural grain" of life—a cross of empowerment rather than a cross of deep, wounded rejection and disconnection.

Dolly Parton was once quoted as saying, "Get down off the cross, honey. Somebody needs the wood." As intelligent beings, we must surely realize by now that if the threatening method of yelling at people about their unworthiness was the answer, then we as a society would not be living in the state of "What are we going to do now?" If the volume of the scream led to the joy of the dream, we would have arrived already, don't you think?

The human body with arms outstretched is uniquely shaped like a cross, for it is our destiny that the truth of the cross set us free. The "truth of the cross" is the deep reality that each of us has the ability many times throughout our lives to resurrect from dying into a new place of deeper living. We go through the resurrection of fear to feelings to freedom when we are willing to leave the old cross on the hill where it belongs.

We have been so programmed like robots that we have missed the subtle clues for us to discover the mystery of who we are.

Have you ever stopped to question why we are taught to "fear the Lord"? Have you ever been afraid of someone? Were you ever afraid of a parent or another relative, and because you were afraid, you just couldn't relax around or truly believe in this person?

This is another message in traditional teachings that works against itself. People are taught to fear the Lord, yet we cannot feel totally connected to anything or anyone we are afraid of. As long as we promote the image of a God that we are supposed to be afraid of, we will be passive people, victims with very little empowerment. We will live a life of codependency, passive and aggressive behaviors, and victimhood.

When you love something with all your heart, you can trust it, believe in it, and give your energy to it. To worship a God you are afraid of drains and disconnects you rather than reaffirming and restoring you.

The only saving we need is to be saved from ourselves. For a person to achieve his or her greatest divine potential, he or she must be saved from the old nature and be born into the new nature. If there really is a devil—a power working against us—it is our own emotional body filled with fears and unresolved feelings that repeatedly attracts to us the same types of rejection, disconnection, and disappointments, until we save ourselves from the necessity of having to learn on the old rugged cross.

How have your beliefs, or lack of them, been working in your life up to this point? Take time to write out your fears and list each of them. Truly experience them and ask yourself: Are they mine or fears I have taken from my family or other influences? Are you excited about your spirituality and your purpose? Are you fully living in a place of trust and of knowing that you are magnificent beyond words?

On a deep level, you and I both know that we have been programmed to believe a lot of things about life and God that simply aren't true. If it isn't true for you, yet you are still living as if it were so, then you will never be true to yourself and your life will not be true to you.

Make a list of the ways in which you have been automatically living, either for approval or because of an unwillingness to stop and make a new story.

No Longer Holding Back

I was conducting a memorial service for a young man who was twenty-seven years old when he died. There were many young families at the service, and there must have been at least eight babies and several small children. Before the service started, I noticed that just about all the babies were crying. They were like a small choir. I opened the service by saying to everyone how grateful we could be to honor the crying in the room. The babies were expressing grief because they could feel the pain in the room.

How fortunate we were to have them give us permission to cry. At this point, no one had taught them to hold back. At this point, no one had wronged them or told them big girls need to be strong or big boys don't cry. No one had gotten to them yet to teach them to hold back their feelings. They were our teachers, and the moment I acknowledged them, the room became quiet. Now we could all feel our sadness, our fear of deaths, and our emotions in different forms, and there was no reason to hold back.

In fact, the more we hold back our authentic feelings, the more we hold back our authentic selves.

How interesting that most of us start life as toddlers singing this song:

> If you're happy and you know it, clap your hands.
> If you're happy and you know it, clap your hands.
> If you're happy and you know it and you really want to show it,
> If you're happy and you know it, clap your hands.

We were not taught to sing about other kinds of feelings: If you're gloomy and you know it, clap your hands. If you're angry and you know it, clap your hands. If you're fearful and you know it, and you really want to show it, if you're fearful and you know it, clap your hands.

Years ago I had a client, Clare, who was a great mother. She had two young girls who were almost teenagers, and they did many projects and went on many outings together (she had been divorced for a long time). She came to see me because she was starting to worry that something was wrong with her, because when she was in the kitchen with her girls, she became an entirely different personality. In all other areas, she was lighthearted, fun, and open, but in the kitchen with her kids, she would yell at them as they were making muffins and often hurt their feelings.

I closed my eyes and could see an image of her mother with her in the kitchen. I could see little Clare being so heartbroken because her mom was being so mean to her in the kitchen. I looked at her and said, "This is how your mom treated you. When you forgive your mom and yourself, when you feel the feelings of the little girl within you, you will be free from the need to continue to repeat this pattern." She woke up just from this one conversation and went home and worked on her pattern. Since then she has been free and has lived like an eagle, no longer distracted by feelings that were truly not hers.

We often do this in our lives, and we are so asleep to it. We carry energies we adopted from our parents or other big people when we were little, and we relive them over and over until we are willing to have an insight ("IN sight") about them. We must be willing to feel the feelings and then acknowledge the feelings so the reality can change. Once the dynamic is brought to the surface, we will be free of it forever.

Like Clare in the kitchen, are there experiences happening in your life right now that are not expressing the true you? Go into the experience and see if this way of being does not reflect a parent, a teacher, or someone you knew rather than who you are.

We often are determined to make change hard. I once saw a couple that was having major problems because the wife did not want to clean the house and the husband did not think it was his job. Except for this one thing, they told me, they were very happy. I said to them, "You can spend years in therapy, or you can pay a cleaning lady. A cleaning service will by far be a lot cheaper and take a lot less time." Somewhere they had learned that it is easier to leave a relationship than it is to figure out a solution. As you grow wiser you realize that leaving something you don't want to deal with only creates a life that doesn't deal you what you could have experienced. Even if you leave something to avoid facing the fear, you will face it again for the fear is within you and, until you face it, you cannot replace it.

We often carry feelings of anguish and rage without even thinking and feeling them through. The solution, it seems, is always easier than the problem.

From the very beginning of our lives, our emotions seem to be left to the discretion of the people who surround us. We are told from the very beginning what is appropriate or inappropriate for little girls and boys to feel. In most of our culture, we are taught not to feel.

We have many masters and leaders telling us at great length that there is a sacred formula that always works. A thought plus a feeling equals an action or result, they might say, yet most of them gloss over the feeling part. They do this because many of them have never learned from or embraced their feelings. Many of them are simply going through the motions without the emotions. They have become robotic in their own way. They have died a little from too much formula and theory and not enough reality through practice.

From my encounters, I sense that many motivational speakers, teachers, and public leaders have not done their own emotional-body work. We are given messages with little or no depth. We are told stories, yet very few contain the experiences of the storytellers. We have self-help, with very little help for self going on. We have mastered the overstimulated intellect and disregarded the deep wisdom of our emotional body. We are not held to a higher standard because they are not living their standards high.

I am reminded of the story of when Mohandas Gandhi was approached by a mother who desperately wanted her child to stop eating sugar. She knew that if Gandhi told the boy to stop eating sugar, he would listen. Gandhi looked at him and told him to come back in six months. Six months later, the mother and son came back, and Gandhi looked at the boy and said, "Quit eating sugar!" The mom was furious. "Why couldn't you have just told him six months ago when we were here? Why did you make us wait so long?" Gandhi replied, "Because *I* had to give up sugar!"

The True Medicine for Fear

From the very beginning of our lives we are not shown mirrors of validation for our feelings by looking into the hearts of our elders, our teachers, and our helpers. Since our feelings are not validated and honored, we begin to doubt the truth that our feelings are telling us. We are trained from the very beginning in subtle ways to not trust ourselves.

When we face it, we will replace it, yet this is not always easy because we carry such deep feelings that we don't even realize they are present within us. I live by the understanding and daily prayer to forgive myself for my trespasses and to forgive those who have trespassed against me. I also live by the longing to be totally impassioned and energized, responsible and empowered for my own life. When we live by this promise, the truth will always reveal itself to us.

A few years ago I was nudged to visit my Aunt B. in North Carolina. My mom and I decided it would be great for me to see her and my uncle, and, even though I was honoring the joy the visit brought to my mom's eyes, I would have been just as happy if we had stayed at my mom's house. I had always adored my Aunt B., yet I never felt any deep connection with her, and I had not been with her for many years. Most of our family gatherings were filled with surface talk, and that was never one of my best traits or most pleasurable pastimes.

I spent the day with my aunt, and, when my mom left the room, my aunt said to me, "I have to say I am amazed at who you have become and all the things you have done with your life." And I said, "Thank you for saying that, especially since I started out early in life with what they did to my mother when I was a little over ten."

Aunt B. said, "What did they do to your mother?" I said, "You mean you do not know?" She said, "No, I have no idea." Then I told her about my mom having shock treatments at the institution the family had sent her to.

The moment Aunt B. told me she did not know was the moment I was forever free of a feeling I had held against her all of my adult life. I was not conscious of this feeling, but deep down I resented that someone I had admired so much as a child would have let anyone harm my mother. I had always thought Aunt B. was very empowered and spoke her mind, so the story did not add up. All the while the story could not add up because it wasn't a real story.

Today we are the best of friends, and I can't imagine my life without her actively in it. We can be free if we allow it to be. Perhaps you may be holding onto a story that is not true, yet it is keeping you from truly moving forward. Take the moments to visit some of the energy or lack of energy you may have with other people or family members.

The true medicine for fear is trust. The key solution to our misery is trust. The answer to the greatest problem is the ability to trust that the answer existed before the problem.

But how do we get there from here? How do we move from *nowhere* to *now-here*?

I remember calling my father many years ago and asking him about the time change. I wasn't sure whether I needed to set my clock an hour forward or an hour back. After he so confidently gave me his answer, I questioned him, stating, "Are you sure?" Being the subtle character that he was, my dad said to me, "Why did you call me if you did not plan to believe the answer I gave to you?"

This experience has stayed with me most of my adult life, for I think of it in a deeper way. He was right, of course. Why would I call upon him if I did not have faith and trust in his answer?

Because of my various experiences with him in my youth, my father had rarely witnessed my total trust in him. I had seen him respond to so many events in such a reactive and insane way that I could never completely let go around him. It took his death to open my heart and fully engage in the gifts he had offered me. He gave me the ability to communicate with anyone, to connect immediately with strangers, (this is definitely a skill), the openness to always seek a solution, the strength to persevere, and the ability to move beyond no as the final answer and discover what was before me.

This experience with my father touched me, yet I was guided to take it to yet a deeper level. What about my Creator, my God? Why do I call upon this amazing presence if I am unwilling to believe in the answers that I receive? Why do we take time to pray if we do not trust our answers? And why would we not totally trust that which we are made of? We will listen so quickly to the opinion of anyone else even though he or she may not model the answers we are seeking.

In order to understand fear, we must first accept the lack of understanding that inhibits trust. For centuries, many writers have stated that the opposite of fear is love. This is a powerful statement, yet from my life experiences and from my experience as a spiritual leader for most of my adult life, I would say that the opposite of fear is trust. Where there is trust, fear is not leading the way by being in the way. Even with the subtle appearances of fear, you will not be stopped. You might feel the sensation of fear, but it will not hold you back. You will believe in your Creator enough to keep moving forward.

You can love many things and still be afraid of them, yet when you trust with all your heart, fear dissipates into the nothingness from which it came. Our lack of trust creates within us an energy that prevents us from truly living and that causes us to die from the inside out, for it is the soul's natural tendency to trust.

Fear of the Dark

Why are we afraid? Many of us know that there are two natural fears: the fear of falling and the fear of loud noises. These fears are innate, lying dormant within us and surfacing throughout our lifetimes. In addition to these two fears, we have instinctive and intuitive responses to situations, people, and places that tell us we are or could be in danger. Our GPS—God-Personalized System—will guide us in any direction at any given time if we trust to listen.

Most of our adult fears come from the very beginning of our lives because our elders and family systems do not seem to have the knowledge, patience, or wisdom to teach us not to be afraid of the dark. At an early age we are discounted and dismissed because we are being "big babies," afraid of the dark. We are often scolded, reprimanded, and invalidated because we are afraid.

Even the adults who do not criticize a child's fear of the dark still approach it at the surface level. They still want to fix it with a nightlight. Rarely does anyone ever delve into the emotional feelings and the real reasons for the fear. We sugarcoat the feelings and then wonder why our children grow into adults who use sugar consumption to cope with feelings. Not long ago I did a shamanic house blessing and a little girl showed me her room and she pointed out the stones she had in a dish near her head that helped her with her bad and scary dreams. As I blessed the house, I incorporated a few lines that involved her and told her not to be afraid of her dreams. She said she wanted to be an artist and I asked her if she could possibly see that the dreams were images for her to paint rather than to fear. She has not ever "had a bad dream" again but dreams that support her greater dreams. An open heart allows us to truly see.

Thus, in our early years we go from trusting that our lives will be taken care of to being deeply rooted in fear. We begin to be invalidated at an early age and therefore spend most of our adult lives invalidating our true feelings of fear and darkness and being in relationships with people who mirror back to us our own invalidation. With this as our early foundation, we somehow, through an influence or the lack of one, make a decision that our Creator does not hear us, does not care about us, and is certainly not interested in what we have to say and pray.

We start very early to project onto our Creator this disconnection of not being heard, not being important, and not being recognized.

We believe from an early age the negative influencers who tell us that our God cannot and will not listen to us.

In the biblical Creation story, we are told that God created the light and the dark, and it was good. Yet how does this get so overlooked, when it is right at the very beginning of this sacred book? Light and dark are equally good and important enough to have been created in the first place.

We begin to die from the inside out when we promote separation by dismissing half of our lives in the darkness. We begin to die a little from the very beginning, because we cannot understand that greater light comes from owning the darkness and that greater joy comes from deep sadness.

Often people will comment on my deep belly laugh and how they love to hear my laughter. After acknowledging the compliment, I quickly say to them, "It came from deep cries, deep pain, and deep self-reflection." My deepest joys come from sitting in my own darkness and learning that there is no reason to be afraid.

We want to rush through the "not so good" feelings to get to the happy place; we do not understand that you cannot rush the process.

When we rush the feelings of sadness, anger, disappointment, or rage, we are not able to get the full benefit of having the feelings in the first place. When we embrace the feelings, it leads us to greater insights and wisdom, shape-shifting our current reality into something much deeper and perhaps even magical.

Last year I led more than 200 people in our spiritual community through a seven-week study program based on a bestselling book about going from darkness into the light. It was fascinating to witness how most people couldn't wait to get through the first two chapters about darkness. So many commented on how they wanted to get to the "good stuff."

As long as we disassociate from one-half of our feelings, we will continue to only half live, and we will die a little, for we have not truly lived with the full capacity of who we are created to be. It is not feeling our feelings that creates problems for ourselves; it is denying our feelings over time that causes our true selves to be denied.

Take the time to write down the ways that you are denying yourself by denying the feelings you are having and discounting. What do you recall about your early years, and how were your feelings either honored or denied? In what ways do you currently treat yourself and others differently from how you were raised?

Ask yourself these two questions that a colleague once asked me:

1. How has your way of avoiding your fears and feelings been working for you thus far?
2. What is the payoff is keeping things the same?

When we live daily with what we cannot swallow, we usually live a life half empty in which we are passive and often wallow.

Since we did not develop an immune system early in life to process the light feelings and the dark feelings, we are weak and vulnerable by the time we are told that there is God and there is a devil and both of them want us. Not only do they want us, but they have immense power over us and we should be afraid. If we are not afraid, then we should be afraid of not being afraid. Many evangelists will stand at the front of a room and tell people to fear God and be afraid. Their deepest fear, if they are truthful, is that we will trust God. For if we learn to trust God, we will no longer be dying a little, and we will no longer need some greater person to tell us whether we are okay. We will thrive in knowing our own sacred creation story.

When we are supposed to be continually afraid, we become susceptible to needing someone to save us, for by this time we believe that separation exists. We believe that we cannot trust ourselves, for we want good and bad things. We cannot trust our bodies, because we are coming from a duality of good and evil. We cannot trust our Creator unless we are doing really good things, and anything short of that is probably the devil's influence.

Note that *devil* is *lived* spelled backward. If we continue to live by old man-made laws without a paradigm shift, we will continue to be held in bondage. We will continue to live against the grain of our lives and will feel the splinters along the way.

How does a false belief in a devil cause us to have *lived* rather than be totally alive?

My Aunt S. was an extremely talented person. Today she would be recognized as a savvy, culturally creative person. She could do anything she set her mind and heart to do. One area that she was not able to master, however, was her feelings of guilt about divorce from her first marriage. She and her first husband divorced, and she could never forgive herself because she was unforgivable in the eyes of the church. She believed that she had failed God and that the devil had come into her heart.

Even though she later married an amazing guy and had an incredible family, she could never *live forward*. Her past became her future over and over.

Her belief that the "devil made me do it" led her to the countryside, where she took her own life. She died for no other reason than a traditional doctrine made up to exert ultimate control over humanity.

Our lives cannot truly move forward until we totally take responsibility for our actions. If we believe a power is always working against us, then we will always be vulnerable to blaming outside circumstances. We will continue to promote a life without choice, and we can say we were tempted rather than that we chose the event that caused the effect.

We must stop buying into traditional thinking that tells us two distinct powers in our lives work in the opposite direction and that if we make the "right" decision, we will be saved.

Trust Is a Muscle

How do we go from fear to feeling to freedom? This is not only an imperative question, it's part of the inner voice that is always asking us to be more. Like you, I have moments when I ask myself, *Can the me of my becoming overcome the me that wants to be stuck in a rut?*

Trust is a muscle. It has to be exercised to develop strength.

Many years ago, in order to become a successful athlete, I was required to work out in the weight room three or four days a week. When my coach first took me into the weight room, I went for the heaviest weights that you could lift. I jumped right into those weights with no hesitancy and therefore strained my back because I had taken on too much at one time, and in doing so I had hurt myself.

I did not allow my muscles to build slowly by stretching a little, then relaxing, stretching some more, and relaxing so that they could truly develop and be strong.

Trust requires "wait training" as well. It's the same concept as weight training, just a different spelling.

If you have not been able to trust your Creator and trust your life, it is too much to conceive of being able to totally trust both all at once. It's too big a step at one time. When you pray, or call in your good, you need to learn how to wait and exercise the muscle of trust. Do not kid yourself; there will be moments that your doubt and fear will want to negate your faith. However, the only way to develop the trust muscle is to use it, and each time you wait, you will begin to see how the things that you have dreamed or called in or prayed for will become your reality. I love the statement "A miracle is what happens when you wake up in your life one day and you are there, and you don't recall all the necessary steps that got you there."

My Most Defining Transformative Moments

Two of my most defining moments of transformation from fear to feeling to freedom happened in my forties. When I met the true love of my life, I knew that my relationship with her was too amazing to keep a secret. I could not allow the innuendos that had occurred in my previous relationships, when my mother would play investigator and try to figure out how good a friend each woman in my life was.

One day on the phone, my mom asked me something about my new friend Barbara, and I asked her why she was interested. She told me she could tell I had a new friend and then asked, "Is it a man or a woman?" Well, I was no longer willing to fluff off that question and change the subject. I had become really good at avoiding what was being asked—but not today. That day, I felt the fear and the feelings, and I was ready for my freedom. I was tired of being tired and drained from not being real with the woman who had given me life. I was ready to be born and to stop dying from lying.

I was not a person who had certain types and colors of lies (i.e., white lies and shades of gray lies). I had always believed in the practice of telling the truth, but not about this. I might die if I told the truth, for that was the memory that lay deep within me, that had cost my mom so much at an early age and had also led my grandmother to part with me at the pearly gates. I simply couldn't do it anymore. To lie was to die energetically.

So I told my mom I would call her later. I called her back that afternoon, and when she answered, I was sitting in my bedroom. I said, "Hold on, mom, I need to close the door." I needed to create a container around me, for I was facing my deepest fear for the first time in my life. Closing the door was so symbolic for me, for I created my own closet to comfort myself, and I had lived in the closet with my family of origin way too long.

I said, "Mom, do you love me?" She said, "Well, of course I do." I said, "Will you always love me?" and she replied, "Yes, of course I will." And then I said, "Even if I love a woman?" and she said, "No matter who you love, I will always love you. You are my daughter and I will always love you." And then I said, "Well, let me tell you about BB. She is the greatest love I have ever known."

The rest, as they say, is history. Today my mom feels she has two daughters rather than one, and I am thriving, for I am not dying every day from the shadow of having a mother I was keeping secrets from. Most important, what a joy to have a mother I trusted enough to let her see me and know me.

Shortly after this tremendous miracle of love in action, I was approached by my office assistant to schedule my picture being taken for our spiritual community directory. She said she would be happy to schedule my appointment and include Barbara also. I felt that feeling again. I was shutting down, so I said, "What did I do last time?" and she said, "That was five years ago, and you weren't with BB then." I heard myself say, "Well, that was convenient!" How discounting and nonempowering is that?

Then I realized I was going back to old patterns of fear and not allowing the feelings to be acknowledged, so I told her to book the appointment. There we were, in living color, for everyone to see. We were dressed in matching colors, and we were indeed a couple. We were now living out loud.

This was an incredible insight for me. As an adult, I knew that everyone in my community was very comfortable with me and BB. We had been open and had not intentionally ever hidden our relationship, but the inner child in me was terrified. I knew I had to dig deeper.

Because of this discomfort, I knew I had more emotional work to do, so I volunteered to speak to a new membership class. I told them that I truly love the teachings of Unity because it was the only spiritual community in my twenties that had accepted me as a gay woman. I told them that Unity had saved my life. Even though I was sharing this story as an adult and I knew they would accept me as I am, inside I was trembling. I could tell that my physiological self was changing from this discomfort, and I kept waiting for some of the forty-four people there to walk out. No one did.

So the next Sunday I told the entire congregation with song and words, and I received three standing ovations.

I was facing the fear, feeling the feelings, and getting a taste of authentic freedom. I was walking into my life by walking deeper through my life.

The next week, a producer from Lifetime Television called me and said she had heard about me. They were doing a segment on *The Balancing Act* about empowerment and would I like to do something on the show for a five-minute segment? Here came those feelings of being terrified again. Oh no, not national television!

So I said, "What about my years of drinking and my success with sobriety?" and she said "Well, that's nice." Then I said, "I could talk about my years as a shamanic practitioner and the miracles I have seen," and she said, "We'll keep talking." Then I got it. Okay, here it is: I am to tell my story on national television that I was discovered in my youth to be having a same-sex relationship, and she shouted, "That's the one!"

From my mom to my spiritual community to national television —my curtain was now open and there was no going back. These moments of moving from fear to feelings to freedom gave me the energy and the passion for living beyond my wildest imagination.

Born to Fly

One of my most teachable moments occurred when I first heard the story of the naturalist and the eagle.

A naturalist was visiting a farm one day and was surprised to see a beautiful eagle in the farmer's chicken coop. Befuddled, the naturalist asked, "Why in the world is that eagle living with chickens?"

"Well," answered the farmer, "I found an abandoned eagle's egg one day and laid it in the coop, and a chicken adopted it and raised the creature after it hatched. It doesn't know any better; it thinks it's a chicken." The eagle was even pecking at grain and strutting awkwardly in circles.

"Doesn't it ever try to fly out of there?" asked the naturalist, noticing that the bird never lifted its gaze.

"No," said the farmer, "I doubt it even knows what it means to fly."

The naturalist asked to take the eagle for a few days for experiments, and the farmer agreed. The scientist placed the eagle on a fence and pushed it off, bellowing, "Fly!" But the bird just fell to the ground and started pecking. He then climbed to the top of a hayloft and did the same thing, but the frightened bird just shrieked and fluttered ungraciously to the barnyard, where it resumed its strutting.

Finally, the naturalist took the docile bird away from the environment to which it had grown accustomed and drove to the highest butte in the county. After a lengthy and sweaty climb to the top with the bird tucked under his arm, he peered over the edge and then said gently, "You were born to soar. It is better that you die here today on the rocks below than live the rest of your life being a chicken. It's not what you are."

With its keen eyesight, the confused bird spotted another eagle soaring on the currents high above the bluff, and a yearning was kindled within it. The naturalist threw the majestic beast up and over the edge, crying out, "Fly! Fly! Fly!"

The eagle began to tumble toward the rocks below, but then it opened its seven-foot wings and, with a mighty screech, instinctively began to flap them. Soon it was gliding gracefully, climbing in ever higher spirals on unseen thermals into the blue sky. Eventually, the mighty eagle disappeared into the glare of the morning sun. The bird had become what it was born to be.

The truth is that we are all eagles, yet if we allow our fears to dictate our reality and we live like chickens, we clearly will be chickens.

You may have accepted the chicken position in your own life, yet each of us is born to be an eagle; we are born to fly.

Ideas to Process and Integrate

~∾⦵∽~

The truth is that the fear will return time and again until the individual goes deep inside and does not hold back.

What fears do you currently carry, and where did you learn them? Write out each fear, and then write beside them what your life would be like without them holding you back. Be willing to accept that, even though you may always feel the sensation of the fear, it does not have to stop you in your tracks. Feel the sensation, own it, and move forward.

We will continue to die a little every day until we move from fear to honoring our feelings to freedom.

We go through the resurrection of fear to feelings to freedom when we are willing to leave the old cross on the hill where it belongs.

The only saving we need is to be saved from ourselves.

When we embrace the feelings, it leads us to greater insights and wisdom, shape-shifting our current realities into something much deeper and perhaps even magical.

What are your deepest fears? List them one by one and give yourself a few hours to really greet them, name them, and own them. Once you have finished this process, set aside half an hour to be uninterrupted in a quiet space. Play soft music if it helps you relax, but not music with lyrics, for the words will be a distraction.

Go into your inner awareness of quiet and ask your Creator or guides to bless you with your sacred warrior shield. Whatever it is, accept it and give thanks for it. You will carry this shield in your mind and heart each time a deep fear presents itself. You will use it until the fear dissipates.

Guess what? Each time you grow deeper into the greatest dreams of your life, your fears will knock on your inner door again. Own them and dust off your shield and use it again. This time it will happen more quickly, and the transformation will be less tedious.

How are you sabotaging your gifts and talents? What would you do, be, and share if you had not told yourself you couldn't, either by your own limitations or someone else's? How do you continue to sabotage your good?

How do you hold back with the people closest to you? What stories in your life do not add up? Are they real, or are they only what you have held as being true? Are your wanting and your being going in the same direction? Please write in your journal how this is so.

3

The Secret to Your *God-Personalized* System

Step Three: How to Restore All Parts of Your Soul and Move from Disconnected and Drained to Energized and Impassioned

How do you want to live? With all parts of the soul complete.
Do you want to be fully awake or half asleep?
Do you want to be totally alive or nearly dead?
Do you want to live from an open heart or a closed heart?
Do you desire to be vibrant or drained?

In a world that is very much asleep, we often forget that it is possible to live with an energy and a vibrancy that reflects our natural expression of nature.

The word *nature* is derived from the Latin word *natura*, or "essential characteristics, essence, disposition," from *natus*, having been born (*Merriam-Webster's* dictionary).

In 1991, when I pioneered my own spiritual community in Stuart, Florida, I wrote the following declaration: "This is the greatest moment that you and I have ever lived. We have never been better, or greater, or more alive than we are right now. You see, as long as we believe there was a better yesterday or that tomorrow holds for us some guarantee, we are missing out on the greatest moment we will ever have, and that is right now. Right now is where we have the power to change our minds, to have a new thought, or to let go of something we no longer want because we truly are empowered individuals."

Regardless of our faith or lack of it, no matter how limited we have been in our beliefs, the magic of life is that in one instant we can be saved—not saved according to some glorified doctrine, but saved from our ways of playing small. We can be saved from not being totally alive. We can be saved from dying while we are living.

At any given moment, we can either be an eagle or a chicken. At any given moment, we can either be living more or dying more. At any given moment, we can be either a full participant or a pretender. At any given moment, we can be like either a thriving tree or a wilted plant.

I have always appreciated the song "Amazing Grace," and I truly believe in God's grace being amazing. I believe it not because someone told me that this is the case; I believe it because I have seen it with my own eyes and open heart. Yet for a long time I was a skeptic as a result of the religiosity, separation, and judgment I witnessed in my early years. I had distanced myself from some of the music, like the song "Amazing Grace," because it reminded me of the times I was told to be a victim and be unworthy. I used to have difficulty accepting the words "a wretch like me." I did not feel like a deplorable, unfortunate, and unhappy person. Somehow I knew that these sacred spiritualist tunes were like ancient chants, and I did not want to chant songs that held me in bondage.

Yet if you look into the depth of the song, which I have learned to do with so many of these old tunes, the story is magnificent. The story is about amazing grace.

John Newton was living a life that he had accepted as familiar. He was following the path of his father as a boat captain who brought slaves to America. He spent many years doing this because he longed for more in his life, but rather than follow his own GPS (God-Personalized System), he followed the expected path. He followed the path of doing what others had done. One evening, when there was a terrible storm, he and all the others aboard feared for their lives. He truly thought he would die. When his physical life was spared, he had a spiritual awakening and his old self died.

He wrote the song "Amazing Grace," one of the most popular songs ever written. He allowed his true self to be restored. He accepted his life challenges, which one day restored the parts of the humanity that he had lost.

What is your amazing grace story? What storm in your life keeps recurring in order for you to die in the way that isn't you so that the real path of your life can reveal itself? How have you followed the path or desire of others when deep within you knew it was not right for you?

Near-Life Experiences

We spend millions of dollars to read or listen to stories about people who have had near-death experiences. We are fascinated by people who validate the religious or spiritual lessons we have learned since childhood about the golden gates of heaven or who offer new ways of "seeing" heaven.

I am much more fascinated with near-life experiences, however. I do not know what happens when we die. I have a sense of it, yet no deity or God has told me to tell you what happens for sure. As a spiritual leader, I am going to continue to leave that mystery to my Creator. I am more interested in what happens while we are living than I am in spending my life in the unknown of what happens when we die.

I am more interested in not dying while I am living. I am more interested in teaching and facilitating processes that encourage people to have more life experiences rather than near-life experiences, or almost fully living experiences.

Near-life experiences are the times you wanted to say how much you loved someone but were afraid of what he or she would think of you. Near-life experiences are waiting and waiting before you truly share with another human being who you are, because you are going to wait and see what the other person will do first. There are so many men and women who never reveal what they mean to each other, for they are waiting to see if they are safe or secure, and they never get to experience the joy of the present moment.

Near-life experiences are all the times you edited yourself or held back out of a concern of what someone might think of you. Near-life experiences are endured by the writers and singers and artists who are waiting for "someday"—you know, the day that never comes—in order to express their gifts and talents. Near-life experiences happen to all the people who live their lives because that's the way they have always done it. Near-life experiences are undergone by lots of people who have decided never to love a person again or never to have a pet again because they don't want to have a broken heart again. They would rather develop hardening of the "ought-teries"—they are the rigid and the nearly dead.

Near-life experiences are accepted by people who live in square boxes rather than in the inclusivity of circles. Near-life experiences happen to people who talk yet do not walk their philosophy. Near-life experiences are the state of being of people who have stopped laughing at themselves and the self-made rules, who have stopped being childlike and are old long before they are even in their thirties. People who have near-life experiences are metaphorically like people who work in a government office that interface with the public and order others around with the tonality of a prison warden; they repeatedly remind you to stay behind the line. Near-life experiences mean that people have never learned how to color outside the lines or draw new lines in the sandbox.

The Energetics of Grief and Loss

By the time I was in my late thirties, I had walked through or around a significant number of life experiences. I was fortunate that as a child I had all my great-grandparents, all my grandparents, and even great-aunts and great-uncles. So by the time I reached twenty years old, I had already said good-bye to so many people who had died. Although I was blessed to have known and loved so many folks, I had dealt with major grief time and again when I was still too young to face so many tragic changes.

I was used to grieving, and I was used to loss. This doesn't even include all the animals that I lost along the way. Some were lost through age, and some through tragic accidents; however, the loss was the loss itself, not the way in which it happened.

I started noticing in my late thirties that the pep in my step was becoming faded. Up until that point, regardless of the situation, circumstances, challenges, or anything else, I had always been the type to get up, get going, get moving, and move on. Whether I had gotten drunk as a teenager and run my car into a tree or into a transfer truck going sixty-five miles an hour on the highway, I had always gotten back up. I drank so much in my teens and early twenties and had so many car accidents that many of my guardian angels sought new assignments. I really think I am the one who gave the auto industry the idea of off-road, all-terrain vehicles, for driving a car while under the influence and keeping it between the lines was not practical to me.

Thank God within me for a sober spirit! I was having way too many near-life experiences. I was showing up, yet spiritually I wasn't growing up. We must move from our knowing to our growing to our showing, and I wasn't doing that. I would simply dust off my feet and my heart, get back on my horse, and continue on the trail.

What I did not realize is that some of my past had never been felt, experienced, and transformed. You might say I glossed over a number of events or drank on top of them. I responded to too many events with a cliché, a bumper sticker answer, or a good quote by Deepak Chopra, Wayne Dyer, or Marianne Williamson—always someone other than myself—to sugarcoat the reality of pain.

There was something about me that was changing, and the best way I can describe it is to say that I had a soul ache. My get-up-and-go just got up and went. I was determined not to share the pain with my dearest friends, for sharing it would make it real, so I kept it to myself.

I was having a series of near-life experiences and was often numb from the outside in. My life turned around 180 degrees when I did a soul retrieval and received a lot of energy back into my body that I had lost. I became more grounded, like a tree with roots that would sustain me through all situations. I became more authentic and more alive. My life turned around when I stopped being whatever someone else wanted me to be and started practicing being me. Yes, I mean *practice*. After a lifetime of being a chameleon and being everything to everyone, I had to practice a lot to unravel the layers and find my originality again. I was no longer dead on the inside while attempting to be awake and alive on the outside.

We are born as vibrant children full of energy and life force and so magnetic. It is possible that when we die we will very easily have the same amount of energy, if not more, than we had when we were born. My friend Caroline Sutherland states, "Wouldn't it be lovely to die and have someone come in the next morning and find our empty slippers because we have simply moved on?"

We are so programmed in our society and told repeatedly that the more we go through, the less of us there will be. Or people say, "You have gone through so much, I don't know how you do it." We say things like "It's not surprising to me that you are so tired and weary," and we have developed a strong belief system that the more we go through, the older we become. We are robotic, which is not natural, and we are told over and over that God will never give us more than we can handle—as if we go to some type of receiving camp and receive our rations of what will or will not be.

Our God is held accountable for so many things that are not supernatural at all; they are simply unnatural. We blame God rather than take responsibility for our near-life experiences.

We have become a society of robots who believe that to be weary is natural. Write this on the mirror of your soul: Thou shalt not be weary!

I believe very strongly that when we go through challenging and hard times, the opposite of what we're told is actually true—that we have every possibility to keep at least the same amount of energy in our bodies throughout our lives. The more we go through, the more of who we can become reveals itself to us, and the more we walk through, the more energy we will have in our bodies, not less.

I am an energetic being immersed in the vibrant life force of an infinite God who created me. If God thought enough of me to create me, shall I think enough of myself to allow myself to be created?

I have proved this to myself time and again in my life. I remember when my father died and I was in my midforties; there was a time in that space that I was starting to die a little. I was operating from survival mode, and I checked into old patterns of how fatigued I was and how weary with all the other elements that go with grieving the death of a parent. A defining day occurred for me when I decided that I would practice what I had learned in my shamanic studies. I would predetermine myself to have more energy after my grieving had passed, and I would be more dynamic and more on task and more vibrant than I'd ever been before.

This prayer into my future became my truth. To understand soul retrieval, it is first essential to understand and to embody that we are an energy force and an energy field and that we are here to live our entire lifetime as energetic beings. There are many people who do not want you to believe this because a lot of products would not be sold, a lot of pharmaceuticals would not be necessary, and we would expand our cultural reality from being told what to do and living in a box to becoming self-reliant and immersed in the energy of God. We would truly be eagles and thriving trees and would develop such a powerful realization of how great our God can be.

The second thing to understand is that the only way we can walk through various experiences is to somewhat "check out," or leave our bodies. We become naturally anesthetized in order to cope with tragic and shocking experiences. This is why when people go through tragic things, they often cannot get in touch with the memories of those moments in therapy because they literally became nonpresent in their bodies in order to deal with the event and what they were feeling. Our bodies are designed perfectly, so when we experience shock to our system in any way, there is an automatic anesthetized response that allows us to adjust to the change. These are the moments when many people are fragmented, when they were not "at home" but had checked out in order to survive the loss. Therefore, they can't consciously call back the moment, the energy, or the memory because they weren't there. They were not mentally "at home" in their bodies when this shock occurred.

After people have had surgery, been in automobile accidents, or experienced tragic loss, for a year or more they often cannot focus clearly or keep up with what is going on around them. They often double-book appointments or forget to show up for them. They make major changes much too soon. This is really normal in how we cope energetically; however, some people never come back. Thus there is soul loss and fragmentation, and they do not return to being an eagle or a thriving tree.

Finding My Shaman

When I visited a friend and congregant who had tragically lost her husband and found her filled with energy, I was astonished. She explained that a shaman had done a ritual on her and invited the energies of her losses throughout the years to come back into her being. In that moment and that space, because of words and her experience, I suddenly was totally awake.

Later that year, I met Berenice Andrews, also known as Ms. B. On the day of my soul retrieval, she asked me to lie down beside her on the floor, go into a meditation, and imagine a place inside myself that reflected the feeling of going home. As I was meditating, she held my hand to allow the energies of me to be felt by her, and a drum was playing in the background. She had asked me not to use my mind to create images because it could interfere with the work that would happen through me. If I focused on certain images, she might also pick them up in my energy field, and this would get in the way of the images that were deep within me.

During my time in the stillness and meditation, I simply kept holding the feeling of what it would be like to come home to myself. Toward the end I saw myself in my own bedroom at home, rising up out of bed, and I was covered in golden glitter—so much that I became solid, like the Oscar trophy. Once I felt this image, the drumming stopped, and the shaman helped me get up and blew energies into my heart and crown chakras.

Ms. B. invited me to come and sit at the kitchen table. She shared with me the many images she had seen and the number of times I had experienced energy loss in my body. These are a few:

- When I was five, my brother was born.
- At age five, I ate poison and my stomach was pumped.
- When I was thirteen or fourteen, my family discovered my gay relationship, and I became worse than the black sheep—I was shamed and banished. This is when my grandmother Lois was clear and stern with me and told me I would not get into heaven. My cousin Bruce also died around this time.
- When I was seventeen, my shaman envisioned, I was in a crypt with very little energy. This was the year my grandfather John Temple Hayes died. My seventeen-year-old energy was standing there, bewildered, looking over my early teenage energies and hoping that I would wake up. I had already begun to die.

The shaman shared with me many things, and at the end she began to cry and said, "Many spirits gathered around you and told me you are a great spirit, and then you were covered in gold." She paused. "I was overwhelmed."

That encounter changed my life, for I began to see God in a more infinite way. I had truly witnessed how two perfect strangers could tap into a universal field of consciousness together and facilitate a process that brought one of them back to life. I had personally witnessed amazing grace.

I totally changed after this; I was able to release the fear of dying and truly start to live. I was no longer shadowed by the sense that something was missing. I started having dynamic and real life experiences and began vibrating on such a different level. The music was more beautiful, the sky was much bluer, and for the first time in many years, I was at a place of peace. I remembered how much God loved me, and I wept.

I was reminded once again of how our GPS—our God-Personalized System—provides for us exactly what we need when we need it. I had been led to the one person, of the 7 billion people in the world, who could teach me more than I had ever been taught. To this day, Ms. B. still holds the record!

I have been a student, a friend, and a confidante of Ms. B.'s for almost twenty years. This relationship offered me many opportunities to do soul retrieval on many of her clients, for she thought that she knew them too well to be objective, so she asked me to do the ritual instead because I was not aware of their history, their challenges, or anything else in their lives.

One woman had experienced loss when she was rather young from her friend dying in an automobile accident and from all the drugs that the woman had done in her youth. She had also been treated terribly by her grandmother, so to survive she had anesthetized herself and had never totally returned to being in her body. She became awake after a soul retrieval.

Another woman had many images in her life, and I saw them very clearly in black-and-white. I was somewhat surprised when I saw an image in color of a man standing in the corner, and he was laughing and demanding all of my attention. He looked like Archie Bunker from the classic TV show *All in the Family.* I asked her about this, for it made no sense to me, and she said she did not resonate with it, either. I continued to tell her other images I had seen, but I could not let this image in color go, for I knew it had some type of significance.

I talked about it some more and finally said, "Do you know the guy who was on *All in the Family*—he was overweight, obnoxious, and balding?" She said, "Oh, you mean Carroll O'Connor?" and then turned three shades of red. I said, "Yes, Archie Bunker is Carroll O'Connor. What does this mean to you?" She said that many years ago she had a sugar daddy who looked just like him, and there needed to be some closure. He had died, and part of her had died with him. She needed to know that he was okay. She asked me if he was well, and I was able to share with her that the images were happy and carefree and filled with life. She woke up after that.

A man I worked with had never made peace with his role in the military. He had never recovered from being in combat, nor had he recovered from divorcing his wife and leaving his family. He had tremendous life loss, and energetically he had been battling stomach cancer for some time. He was not able to stomach his path. We were able to give him some new insight and new energy, and he lived for many years. He finally found peace.

One of my hardest cases was a woman who had ovarian cancer. I had to wait until she finished chemotherapy because I can feel the effects of people's medication, drugs, or alcohol, and it is too much to bear. When I went into the otherworld reality, the only images I saw were of a hospital or clinic with nurses and doctors. Now, keep in mind, up until this point, every soul retrieval I had ever led people through included many images at various stages of their lives, yet the only images she had were repeated images of hospitals and clinics. She turned white when I told her this, and she revealed to me that she had had seventeen abortions and had never told her husband. Abortions, I have always found, create soul loss, yet her other deep loss was living the lies. I thought she had a few brighter months to live, for she had been able to tell someone her story, her tragedy, and her pain. Her missing parts were returned to her because for the first time in many years she had told the truth. The truth will set us free. For some it sets them free to live; for others it gives them the freedom to physically die.

This is a perfect example of even though we may have societal approval, the deeper question for you to ask of your life is does this meet the approval of your soul? This applies to all of us as human beings.

Another client was in her thirties, had a lack of focus, and wanted a deeper connection with herself. She would always stop just shy of following through with her successes. She had never known financial freedom in her life; she always had "too much month at the end of the money." When I returned from our spirit journey, I shared with her that one of the images I had seen in the nonordinary reality was a stone in the palm of a child's hands. I asked if this meant anything to her.

She became very emotional as she said that this image was of her when she was a little girl. Her father had given her the stone, and at that moment she had made a vow to God and had not kept it. She realized that she had died energetically back then because she had not kept her vow. When we lie a little, we die a little. When we lie a lot to ourselves, we die a lot and become separate from ourselves.

Some people will argue that they only tell "little white lies." They do not understand that lies cannot be coded and are not lessened by being a certain color. A lie will always reveal itself as a truth in the end either as a blessing or a curse. A lie will always find its way to a truism. Anyone who has ever witnessed kinesiology knows that the body will never accept a lie as the truth. When you lie, it drains your energy flow. When you never live as yourself spiritually, mentally, physically, and emotionally, you are living and dying a lot, with a big exclamation mark.

My shaman teacher's client renewed her soul by bringing back into her life the vow she was now ready to pursue, and her life changed dramatically once she woke up and was birthed into her authentic self. She became happy, financially successful, and an energized being.

A very young woman always had excruciating headaches and had suffered a life half lived for many years. In her soul retrieval, I kept seeing images of a church setting. It was a small church in the country, she was holding her hands over her ears, and she was wearing very thick glasses. When I shared this image with her, she began to wail. She had despised going to this church with her grandparents because the minister had sexually abused her. The thick glasses represented her ability to magnify what no one else could see, and covering her ears represented that she could not hear his messages because he did not live in the truth. She began to die from who she was to be because she had amazing intuitive gifts but denied them. She was not seen, heard, or believed as a child, and so she died a little. And then she died a lot. Once these energies were lifted, she was able to wake up and be born to the life that was truly hers.

This is why I love this work so much; you cannot make this stuff up. It is beyond words and language that influence people's minds. In order to do this work, you must first become an open spirit in your own life. Then you can train your heart to be open to receive the images of people's life journeys that make sense only to them. However, before you can visit anyone else's soul journey, you must first have cleared the path for your own. It is not a business card or a title that makes this way possible; it is opening to the way of Spirit. It is learning how to train your mind so that your heart will be open.

I have never seen images that the person I am working with does not understand. There is a reason we have come together in the first place, a kind of divine appointment that we have been assigned. These people become my sacred friends; they are able to receive the disconnected energy back into their bodies and become awake.

Our Inner GPS
God-*Personalized System*

I discovered our inner GPS when I was in my early thirties. I was driving in my car from South Carolina with one of my dear friends. She and I were so busy talking that I failed to turn onto the right highway. Once I realized the error, I had to go several miles around and then all the way back, so we figured it had cost us almost an hour of driving time. When we made it back to where we were supposed to be, we came to a fifteen- or twenty-car pileup. The damage was major. People were dead. My friend and I looked at each other with goose bumps all over us, for we realized that had we taken the right road at the time we had intended, we would have been killed. We would have been right at the front of the pileup.

We were late by an hour and saved for a lifetime. I have never forgotten this. I have continued to live by not being upset in traffic jams or if the car didn't start or if someone dropped by unexpectedly and delayed me. I remind myself that there is something on the highway or on my path that I am avoiding or being spared from. I'm glad the angels and guides are helping me!

When you live by using your own trust muscle, then you truly realize that you cannot keep your good and your blessings away from you.

Many years ago I read this amazing piece by Dr. Ernest Holmes, and it resonated at the deepest level of my being. It has been a constant and an absolute truth in my life. It is, in my humble opinion, one of the very few truths that is a "one size fits all":

MY OWN SHALL COME TO ME

From far and near my own shall come to me. Even now it is coming to me, and I receive it.

My Own is now manifesting itself to me, and I see and know its presence. My Own shall know and respond to me.

The drawing power of that inner Spirit within me is now attracting and drawing into my experience all that is good and perfect. There is nothing within me to hinder nor to delay it.

My Own cannot be kept from me, neither can I keep my good away from me. I receive it now.

I now receive my good.

MY OWN SHALL FIND ME.

My Own shall find me; no matter where I go, it will follow and claim me.

I cannot hide myself from my Own.

My Own shall come to me, even though I deny it; for there is nothing in me that can hinder it from entering and taking possession of my Soul.

My Own is now expressed.

I actually started writing thoughts down about this book, *When Did You Die?* a few years ago, but like so many of you, I was waiting for the right time. The title of the book was given to me while on a spirit journey. I was having yet another near-life experience. Last summer a publicist from Los Angeles shared with me the value and necessity of writing a book with my big message if I wanted to truly affect a world greater than the choir I had been speaking/teaching to before.

I told him that I appreciated his feedback, but I had accepted that a book of this magnitude was not mine to do. I started to explain all the reasons, such as my busy spiritual community, my consulting work, my radio show, and my other nonprofit work. I was good at saying the list, for sure. I was very convincing, and I made it clear to him that my answer to writing a book right now was no.

Two weeks later Rebecca Johnson, a dear friend and a writer and an editor in the Tampa Bay area, visited me at Unity Campus and said we should talk about my book. She had been gently reminding me for a few years that I needed to do it. I just couldn't bear to tell her in the café line that I was going to say no to the book, so I asked her to contact me and we could visit over tea. I was clear that I would meet her and tell her that if God wanted me to write a book, it would be an easier process.

Well, she did not call me. She wrote to a literary agent instead and asked her to help me get my book out in the world, and the rest, they say, is history.

My Own shall come to me, even though I deny it; for there is nothing in me that can hinder it from entering and taking possession of my Soul.

My Own is now expressed.

Signs, Healings, and Revealings

Think of your GPS this way: If you enter the wrong address into your car navigation system to take you home, it will take you where you told it but never get you back to your house. This is how so many people are living their lives. The Creator has given them instructions to get them to their place of destination, but like John Newton, they are not going in the direction they ultimately want to go. Your inner GPS will never lead you to a place where you cannot discover the home within yourself.

When I first started working with my teacher of shamanism, I understood two things: 1) A shaman practices wholeness and sees life through the eyes of infinity; 2) A practicing, awake spiritual being cannot do deep spiritual work by being in a box or doing life the way he or she has always done it.

I was able to see that even though I believe in an infinite God, I was not allowing my infinite God to create new things for me. I had continued to pray about my same problems and my same challenges, and I was unwilling to use my trust muscle. I was continuing to be the chicken of old beliefs rather than flying in my eagle suit.

On one of my spirit journeys, which you might prefer to call a deep meditation, I was asking the question "How can I be free?" The answer I received was an elderly sage giving me a feather. I started to notice that no matter where I was, whatever city or country I might be in, when I started to go back to old ways of thinking and old ways of seeing, I would find a feather or feathers. They would literally fall down from the sky in front of me at times.

One time I was speaking at Bletchley Park in Milton Keynes outside London to an all-day class on stress management, and I was feeling sorry for myself. I doubted that I was where I needed to be, and I was questioning my path. Why am I here talking to these people about topics that are not very deep or interesting to me? How can I really teach stress management when I am not allowed in the courses to talk about being connected to a higher power? The company had made it clear that they wanted to approach the material from a corporate/motivational perspective rather than a spiritual one. I imagine they were afraid they would offend the non-believers. What's the point? I took a break, and when I returned, there were twenty to thirty feathers in the spot where I had been standing to do my talk. It brought me to tears. I became awake and went from a near-life experience to being fully present and engaged in infinity. I became whole.

I shared a few of these feather stories with one of my dear friends, John. He had been following my teachings for a few years, but he, like so many others, had been trained to see God in a box, so at times he thought I was a little "out there." He listened to the feather stories, yet he would comment with "uh-huh . . . uh-huh," which often means "I think you are cuckoo." I was comfortable with that, however, because I *am* a little "out there."

I had shared the feather story with him as we were traveling to Savannah, Georgia. As God would have it, once we reached Savannah, we were driving downtown in his convertible with the top down, and a feather fell into the car. It was sizable, and boy, was my friend shocked! He was speechless, and as we turned the corner, the feather flew out of my hands, and he said, "Oh no, we lost it!" I assured him that it would find its way back, and sure enough, in a few seconds, either that feather or another almost identical feather fell into the car. A God-moment—oh my.

A few months later I got into John's car, and he had several feathers over his visor. He had made one of life's greatest discoveries: You will experience an infinite Creator and amazing life experiences through your own willingness to be coming from an open heart.

That week in Georgia, he named me the Feather Lady, and my feathers have given me comfort, triumph, depth, and many tears of joy ever since.

One of the greatest loves of my life, Sir Digby (all six pounds of a Yorkshire terrier who thought he was a Great Dane) died last year, and after he had walked out of his body and a couple of weeks had passed, I spoke to him. I asked him to send me a sign, saying, "You know the sign I am seeking—I just want to know you are doing well." The next day I was walking on the beach with four friends, and as we walked, we noticed some feathers. They were everywhere—many more than my norm of twenty or thirty within a one-mile walk. I had felt the infinite connection of God. I had transformed a near-life experience to a state of being awake. I was whole.

What symbol or sign can you use as your spiritual GPS reminder? It could be a penny, a feather, butterfly, dolphin, or a rainbow that would show up right when you need a lift. Pick one for your new life experiences so you can begin to look at life through eyes of infinity and wholeness. Pick your symbol by going into a deep meditation and asking your inner awareness to reveal a symbol to you and allow it to show you amazing grace.

As a culture, we have limited our ability to see our Creator by listening to what people say about God. We have an idea or an ideal of the divine based on what a relative told us or what a preacher said when we were little. As long as we believe what we were told about God when we were little, energetically we will always be little, for we must grow into our own understanding of our Creator. As long as we hold a belief that God is little and has little meaning to us, our lives will have little meaning to us. We will experience little moments rather than great moments. It is our destiny to express our own innate, homemade special recipe and reality of God. This is the way to live a true miraculous life.

It is amazing how much we know and yet how little we know at the same time. Astrologers, sages, shamans, wise elders of various tribes, and aboriginal peoples all understand that nature is where the proven essence of God exists. We are born of the earth and to the earth we return, and our connection to God comes through following our own inner rituals and practices that allow us to see God. The presence and power of God reveals itself to us through our ability to see and be with the hidden gifts that lie dormant within us until we become awake. Then we recognize our wholeness. We do not become whole; we simply accept that we are and have always been whole.

My Eiffel Tower

There are a few distinctions I make in my spiritual practices.

When I pray, I speak to God. I actually believe that we are always praying with our words and affirmative declarations.

When I meditate, God speaks to me.

When I go on a sacred journey, I go deep within myself, to my inner sanctuary. I smudge (i.e., burn sage to purify) my environment, myself, and my surroundings, clearing the energy. I cover my eyes with a handkerchief, and I listen to the beat of a drum. I often use the music of Michael Harner—the thirty-minute drum call for spirit journeying. I visualize going down into the earth into the nonordinary reality. I usually start out visualizing a tree, like the tree standing by itself on the grounds of Machu Picchu. I walk up to the tree and go down its roots, entering a space of ancient wisdom. I always ask one question in which I have the intention of seeking clarity and direction.

A few years ago I asked what tool or symbol I needed to become more grounded. I went on a sacred journey and was mindful of being detached from what I might discover.

The image I continued to get was the Eiffel Tower. I began to question myself. I absolutely love Paris, yet I began to question my process—really, the Eiffel Tower? At first I thought, *Of course, it is because the Eiffel Tower was first laughed at and not wanted by a lot of the Parisian people.* I related to that well. Being original often leads to a lot of laughter, nonacceptance, or bullying from others. I knew that path all too well.

I then drew a picture of the Eiffel Tower, and the following Sunday afternoon I saw an article in *Parade* magazine that stated, "Psychics travel from all over the world to be at the Eiffel Tower this weekend"—the same weekend I was gifted the symbol of the Eiffel

Tower—because they believe that the signal at the Eiffel Tower is stronger than most places in the world.

And in that moment I got it: the Eiffel Tower has four legs that keep it centered and grounded. For me these four legs represented the emotional, mental, spiritual, and physical expressions of myself. When I am balanced in these four areas, my signal and intuitive powers are immense.

Thus, the Eiffel Tower became a strong and sacred totem for me, and many images of it grace my home to remind me of the necessity and the benefits of being grounded and centered.

These symbols come to us when we ask for them, and they are uniquely designed to serve us by making a deep connection with us.

We have gone amiss by losing the sacred art of ancient rituals and symbols in our culture. It is evident that we want these rituals and symbols, however, because of the popularity of books by J. K. Rowling and Dan Brown and films such as *Raiders of the Lost Ark* and *Indiana Jones*. We long to understand infinite wisdom through mystical teachings, signs, codes, and symbols.

Many of us have been influenced by such writings as the Bible or the Koran or symbols such as the cross, yet we have been deeply lacking in creating symbols and interpretations of our own.

The archetypes, symbols, and signs that are unique to our own GPS are essential for us to feel connected, tuned in, and energized.

Stories are just stories unless they become our own stories and we can use them, and symbols are simply symbols unless they anchor, heal, energize, or reveal us. The symbols and signs that are revealed to us through our deep meditations are not only ancient medicine; they also work for us because we created them out of ourselves.

A number of years ago while in upper state New York, I was invited to do an energy healing for a woman who had been sick off and on for a long time. As I worked with her, I kept feeling the presence of a very large cow. I said to her, "This is odd to say yet I must tell you there is a cow's energy all around you." She began to deeply cry and stated, "That's Daisy. Daisy was my show cow when I was a little girl. One of the greatest loves of my life." I told her Daisy was still with her and encouraged her to get out an old photo of Daisy and place it where she would see it on occasion. It would keep the invitation of an open heart in front of her and remind her that love never dies. True love brings us to the acceptance of our wholeness.

Spiritual Relocation

Have you ever experienced a spiritual relocation?

I was on a plane recently with a woman who was very agitated, and she kept reacting to the people behind her, asking them not to talk so she could sleep. She kept making remarks that were demeaning to them, and she was acting as if she were sitting in first class rather than in coach. She was acting like a spoiled brat, yet I knew something was going on underneath the layers of anger. Rather than react to her reactions, I sent her silent blessings to wake up.

At one point, I asked her if she knew whether we were changing time zones, with a difference of one or two hours. She looked at me and began to sob deeply. She told me that her husband was having an affair, that she had just made this discovery, and that she was on her way to visit her mom. I said, "So you are having a spiritual relocation?" and she asked, "What does that mean?" I explained to her that a spiritual relocation occurs when we are taken completely off guard because we suddenly lose what we think we had. This loss could be a house, a job, or a relationship. We are shocked by it ending; however, many times we think it has just been taken from us when the truth is that we have not been in it for a long time. It takes Spirit to change it, for we are unwilling to change it ourselves. Thus it is a spiritual relocation. These types of changes usually hurt the deepest yet reward us in the end the most.

She said, "I can see what you mean; my husband would never allow me to cry." So I reminded her that one day she would be on the other side of the pain, and in the future, when a person would not "let" her cry, be herself, have a child, or have a pet, that would be her first clue to "let" that person alone! A Southerner would say, "Girl, let them alone and keep on walking."

What spiritual relocations have you had in your own life? Were you wealthy at one time but now you are not? Did you think you were retired but now find that you cannot be, so you are off to work once again? Did you send your children out into the world only to discover that you are now raising your grandchildren? Did you have a nine-to-five job and the boss suddenly let you go without a clue? Did your spouse shock you by announcing that he or she is no longer happy? Were you totally surprised to hear that you are not healthy when you thought you were?

All these experiences are just a few of the spiritual relocations that have the potential to get us more aligned with who we are destined to be. The biggest challenge with a spiritual relocation is our inability to trust that it is for a greater design or it wouldn't have happened in the first place. As we learn to trust the process, we begin to see from a different angle, and the event strengthens us rather than weakening us and making us weary. We ultimately see that even though we did not have the courage within ourselves to make the changes, the changes not only occurred, they also gave the gift of new changes which gave us our lives back. They opened our hearts up again.

One World and One Heart

We are at a crucial time in our society, for we need more people to connect and become totally alive again. We have a significant amount of soul fragmentation, both as individuals and collectively as we face tragedy and crisis together.

Our nation had soul fragmentation when terrorists attacked the World Trade Center and the Pentagon on 9/11. The World Trade Center was attacked because it was supposedly symbolic of American trade and opulence. We have unresolved brokenness from this tragedy, and since then our economy has been broken. We can act as if the two are not connected, or we can allow ourselves to feel the linkage. What we choose is not an accident, for either we believe we play a part in our own humanity and spiritual connection or we believe that life is random. When we heal our fragmentation and come from wholeness rather than brokenness, we are able to grieve, die, be reborn, and live totally again.

Hurricane Katrina and other tragic losses have also created a great sense of soul fragmentation on our planet. In ancient times, the ritual and consistent practice after an act of nature or other tragedy was to come together and grieve. This practice supported community and prevented it from having deep soul loss and fragmentation.

We have two challenges now. One is that many people have stopped participating in these types of rituals to transcend the pain, and the other challenge stems from the fact that we learn about world losses at a moment's notice. If we are not into the practice of rituals to move us from the pain to the gain, we will continue to be weary as a people and will not step into our greater capacities as a society.

During Katrina and various tsunamis, people from all over the world were responding in grief and feeling the depth of loss. We felt the loss and dealt with it, and now when any community goes through a significant loss, we all learn to participate in a much greater way than we used to. I often attend drum circles and equinox and solstice ceremonies, which align people, and ancient healing techniques, dancing, drumming, and chanting, which open up the heart and reveal us to one another. Also, being in or near water, or even just listening to water, is immensely powerful when we have experienced major losses in our lives and in our culture. Water is the great healer for our emotional body.

We are so aware and informed now, and our losses are no longer localized. We know of losses all over the world, and at any given point through social media, so if you are not into the practice of coping constructively with all these energies and losses, you will become weary, disconnected, and drained. We cope constructively by chanting, dancing, drumming, and, most important, feeling the energies through us so they may pass from us.

We are finally learning that we are one world and ultimately one heart.

Honoring the Soul Path

When I sometimes forget what I sense I might know, or I become weary as a difference maker, or I need a reminder of what I truly believe, I go to the energy of children. Many years ago, on a sacred spirit journey, I sought to understand the energetic qualities of myself, my allies, and my adversaries. I was seeking to be given archetypes that would support me to be aware of the energies that enhance my life and the energies that detract from my amazing life. I went into a deep meditation and sought the attributes that are my energetic drivers.

Energetic drivers in your day-to-day life are like a computer, a tablet, or a smart phone that has so many windows open that it technically slows the process down. When too many windows are running, it uses the battery way too quickly, and the same is true with us. Our batteries get used up way too quickly because these drivers are depleting us and making us weary. So I was searching to understand my drivers, and I connected with the "windows" I was consciously or unconsciously running in my day-to-day life. In simple terms, I discovered my inner qualities, which include my light (what I persist in), my darkness (what I resist), and all the great shadows (probably what I deny yet get to experience until I accept) in the middle.

One of my adversaries was the image of an aged priest named Heremie who, from time to time, would go into a depression, a very sad or drained place. He was feeling disconnected and drained rather than energetic and impassioned. I realized during this discovery that Heremie represented a part of me that I had felt from time to time all my life. Heremie was actually the underneath layer of the life I was attempting to force, called Hurry-Me. *Life, you are not giving me the results I am seeking fast enough, so please Hurry-Me along.* I had learned the ways of my father. *I have waited too long already, and God, where are you, anyway? I have been saying yes since I was five, and now here I am in my forties. When? When?*

So Heremie (Hurry-Me) explained an inner energetic driver I had experienced for a long time, and the medicine for Heremie was to be with children. It is no surprise that at that time, life had brought me back into working at a spiritual community so I could be around all the good and natural medicine of children, since I had no children of my own. Children are so clear that the path is the path, and they are where they are supposed to be.

Naturally, without hesitancy, children say yes, I do, or no, I am not interested. The essence of a child is freedom. Children do not judge or hold back their feelings. They would continue to develop into adults who express the same, yet over the years their tribe and villages discount the right to feel, to affirm, or to walk away. Their natural esteem becomes a lack of self-esteem, for the fundamental value of self is to be. Be life! Most important, be you!

These processes revealed to me the value of honoring the path of my soul and honoring the past, present, and future as the *now* time.

Ms. B. used to read a beautiful writing called "A Ritual for the Path of My Faith" before each weekend retreat and ceremony. Take a few minutes to find the perfect object to represent your current life and faith. Sit comfortably, facing your past and holding your present, and read the following words (you can also record them beforehand and listen to them or use them as a model to make up your own words):

> I face the path of my faith.
> This is the way I've come,
> the journey my soul has taken
> to bring me to where I am today.
> I recall the people I've met on this path,
> teachers all,
> kind or unkind.
> They walked with me awhile,
> showed me their paths,
> and so I bless their teaching.
> I remember events and encounters along the way,
> pleasant or painful,
> always instructive—
> Whatever happened, it was useful,
> and in its own integrity was beautiful.
> But I have learned to follow my own path,
> I have learned where I must go.
> I bless the path of my past.

Still holding the symbol of your present, turn around. You are turning your back on your past and putting it behind you. Continue:

> Holding my present in my own hands,
> I face my future.
> Every day I step forward on an unknown path,

a unique path sprinkled with star stuff
of Spirit.
Past, present, future are one time
and here I am,
where I'm supposed to be—
now and always:
my path is with Spirit.

I would recommend to you, as a student of life who is greatly longing to be an intentional spirit, that you practice this ritual for three months and see how your life changes. Read this ritual every morning before you start your day and make notes in your journal of how your life changes. Your energy will greatly increase from this sacred practice. Imagine! And you will feel less disconnected and drained, more impassioned and energized, and you will be living on the path of *now*.

Your GPS will gladly announce, "You have reached your point of destination."

Ideas to Process and Integrate

~∞∞∞∞∞~

How can you create a definition of your Creator in your life that includes you rather than excludes you? As long as you have exclusionary beliefs, you cannot be in alignment for a thriving and dynamic life. Step into your amazing life by noticing the delays and interruptions in your life and considering them as guidance and support rather than a hindrance.

Begin to see your signs when you need them to become more aware and awake in your day-to-day life.

Write in your journal how you feel. Are you are in the midst of a spiritual relocation, or are you ready to call or pray for one to come? Otherwise write about the one most recent to you. What true change can or did occur?

A shaman practices wholeness and sees life through the eyes of infinity.

Do you see through the eyes of an open heart and trust or through your disbelief? Take time to observe your actions and reactions when the unexpected occurs.

So many doubts and fears and distrust of allowing people to get close to me had to die so I could let people into my heart.

How many people are in your heart?

It is our destiny to express our own innate, home-made, special reality of God.

Stories are just stories unless they become our own stories and we can use them, and symbols are simply symbols unless they anchor, heal, energize, or reveal us.

Create a symbol for yourself as I did with the Eiffel Tower. When you see it, it will immediately anchor you.

❧ 4 ❧

Happy Birthday, *Real* Me

Step Four: How to Be Reborn as the Real You

Many years ago, I heard Dr. Stuart Grayson refer to his hero Carl Jung. He said that Jung had given us great wisdom with the following concept:

First, you must realize you are asleep
Then you die so you can be born.
You cannot be born until you die
And you cannot die until you wake.

Dying and being reborn is such a paradox. Although it is necessary to wake up so we will not continue to die a little every day from our learned way of being robotic in nature, it is also imperative that we allow parts of ourselves to die so the greater self can become realized. I see this often with people in recovery. They have stopped drinking but are still unwilling to give up the misery the drinking used to give them. They no longer apologize about overindulging in alcohol, yet they continue to apologize about their lives.

It amazes me that somehow, through the processes I have written about in the first three chapters, I became in awe of my life—I, the one who could have easily died a physical death because of all the automobile accidents I had or the many times I drank enough alcohol to kill myself.

Each year when another birthday rolls around, I celebrate this journey on many levels: first, that I survived myself long enough to tell these stories, and second, that I actually lived long enough to discover aspects, gifts, and qualities about myself that are beyond my past imaginings.

Instead of singing "Happy birthday to me," I have changed the words to "Happy birthday, real me": "Happy birthday, real me / Happy birthday, real me / Happy birthday, real Temple / Happy birthday, real me."

It's a powerful moment and reflective of so many miracles that have happened and continue to happen in my life. I tell people that I am no different in character and in being than I was when I was a child; I have simply died a lot and been reborn a lot so that I could give myself permission to be the real me.

The real you is not a place you arrive at, a new credential, or a new career. Being the real you means to know inside yourself that there is no holding back, that in every situation of your life you can feel fully expressed. Many people are walking around with unconscious strait-jackets on that prevent them from being truly free. The Civil Rights Movement took off not simply because Rosa Parks was tired of being abused and became brave. She changed the movement because in the way she responded it was as if she was declaring, "This is my seat, and

I am not moving!" Often, the real you and the real me are too quick to give up our seats. We are too quick to back down from what we really believe in. The world changed the day Rosa Parks declared she would not give up her seat.

How would the world change if you said, "My seat in life is to express how animals are wrongly treated" or "My seat in life is to show people how to be thriving and energetic" or "My seat in life is to show people how to have a successful marriage" or "My seat in life is to show people how to be healthy and happy"?

Celebrating the tremendous freedom of the real you means being able to dance and feel and sing while claiming your "seat" in life and being unwilling to give it up.

I remember how surprised I was at my fiftieth birthday party to see more than 200 people singing "Happy Birthday" to me. It was such an overwhelming feeling. There was a huge photo of me as a baby about nine months old, and there was also a photo of me in my forties—what I had become. As I stood there, breathing in all the energy from people from all walks of life, I was able to feel how much of the old me had died so that the real me was starting to come through. So many doubts and fears and so much distrust of allowing people to get close to me had had to die so I could let people into my heart. A heart once guarded was now open to receive and let people in. It was truly a rebirthing experience.

Rebirthing is a strong part of our life experiences that most people have yet to make a connection with. We die often in this lifetime, and we are born again in this lifetime. Just as ocean waves move toward us and away from us with their ebb and flow, so it is with us in our human suits. We have areas in our lives that have died that we need to wake up, and we have areas in our lives that we need to truly bury and put behind us. To be thriving trees, we must honor the value of pruning ourselves from time to time.

The deepest realization of our covenant with our Creator is allowing the new layering of who we are to continue to emerge.

What is currently in your life that you need to prune? Is it time to let go of some relationships that are not changing and growing with you? Is it time to let go of another layer of self-criticism or of being too analytical? Perhaps it is time to prune spending too much time watching television or overindulging in negativity.

"Happy birthday, real you" gets you into the mind-set of the values and promises you continue to make to yourself and others every year of this amazing journey we call life.

Beware of the Influencers

As a spiritual leader and as a human being who has felt very connected to Spirit since I was five, I have always been fascinated with the idea of why people do not change that much. I have also been fascinated with why people become disenchanted and feel disconnected so early in their lives. I totally understood this in the area where I was raised because people had already been so heavily influenced by being told what to do, what to feel, what to believe in, and how life was going to be. "Don't expect too much, and you won't be disappointed" is a mantra I remember all too well. When we have sacrificed our ability to use free will and choice and have given this powerful ability over to preachers, doctors, 24/7 news, and other realities, we can change only as the influencer changes.

These influencers cast a great shadow over us and limit our ability to grow into who we are meant to be. A tree with another tree hovering over it will eventually bow down. The same is true for us as we continue to give up our seat, our place in this life. All of a sudden life does not have a place for us. Our childhood dreams and goals become nothing more than shadows left on our trail.

The influencers do not want us to change, for it is to their benefit that we stay in a box. I cannot drive for three miles without seeing billboards that say where the best emergency room is waiting for me or stating that if I am feeling a certain way, it is probably a stroke. We have simply lost control of the innate ability to listen to the gift of our own intuition about our healings and revealings.

This is like my own life when I was growing up. I had great intuitive powers living in the country, where it was quiet and I felt such a strong connection with nature. When I moved away to more urban areas, such as Greenville, South Carolina, and then Fort Lauderdale, Florida, with all the busy and constant stimulation I began to lose some of these innate experiences and responses. I moved northeast to Jupiter, Florida, on a six-acre parcel of land, and in this environment I was able to wake up those gifts again. Now I have spent so many years with the quiet inside me that it doesn't matter where I live, for the real me is developed enough to be everlasting.

The same can be said about all the traffic and noise of ideas that we hear day after day. If the real you isn't developed enough to listen to the quiet inside, you will continue to live a life that is not really yours. You will be the chameleon of everything and everyone.

We are constantly bombarded to think a certain way by the "isms" created by the influencers. It is to their advantage that we are robotic and do not question what we are being told. We are talking about trillions of dollars spent on medicine, donations to certain churches to buy a ticket to some promised place called heaven, and advertisements on our televisions, radios, tablets, and phones that tell us to be afraid. We are told there isn't enough or that you won't have it unless you buy (fill in the blank). It is not an accident that our country is in debt by trillions of dollars. We are approaching life as if we are broken and need to be saved, and therefore we as a society are reflecting this as well.

A broken nonauthentic person is usually brokenhearted, waiting for something new to save him or her, and broken financially as well. Our society and culture must die so we may wake up and get back into using our minds and hearts and intuition to guide our decisions.

We are bombarded with messages by the following influencers:

Because the Bible says so
Because the preacher says so
Because the doctor says so
Because my parents said so
Because the billboard tells me so
Because the commercials on TV, radio, and the Internet say so
Because someone else says so

When we surrender to what others say we should be and do and it does not feel inherently right for us, we give up the seat of the real me. Whatever your influencers are telling you, make sure they have manifested in themselves what you are seeking.

Life Advocacy

At times I am rather shocked that I have become a life activist. Life was very confusing at such a young age that I attempted on some level to destroy my life by abusing alcohol or by longing to be me but being terrified to be so. I took my own life for granted for so long. I felt so out of place externally, never belonging, that I projected this sense of not belonging onto everyone and everything.

I had to learn to dare to reach higher than just surviving this life. I had to learn how to transform from surviving to thriving. I had to evolve from just getting by in life to truly giving the real me to the world.

We must aim higher in order to discover our real selves. In my early days of sobriety, I did not want to just be a person who could survive this life and not drink; I wanted to dare myself into the belief that one day I would be a role model of healthy sobriety. I wanted to accept that it was not my path to be a long-term drinker but that there was a better, more enlightened path for me, and I was not willing to make it a struggle. I had given enough years of my life to apologies and my struggle with alcohol that I did not want to keep giving more years of my life to this.

My life over the years had become one big apology in one form or another, and on a deep level it had to be that way, for I did not know who I was. I always had to apologize for my life, for I had given up my seat long ago. My life had not been mine for a very long time, for I simply did what the influencers told me so I could keep peace around me. I quit drinking, which was a relief, yet as I look back, I realize that this was the easiest part of sobriety. Many people stop drinking yet never spend the time necessary to change the inward ideas that they were trying to drown in the first place.

I had to discover all the emotions I had drowned with alcohol and go through an entire rebirthing process. The alcoholic needed to die so the sober woman could live. The same is true with other experiences when we are healing the energy we have given to the influencers. There must be a spiritual awakening—a name-it-and-claim-it attitude. In other words, behind every apology or awareness of how we have allowed ourselves to be weak, weary, and influenced, we must see the deeper truth: *I allowed it.*

Forgiveness is not complicated. What is complicated is the unwillingness to accept responsibility for our actions and choices and the desire to avoid forgiving ourselves. Once we forgive ourselves for being less than dynamic, magnificent, miracle workers; once we forgive ourselves for settling for less than what the covenant from our

Creator states our lives will be; and once we forgive ourselves truly inside and out, we will no longer attract the same actions with others, so we can practice forgiveness with them.

I allowed this. I forgive myself, for I allowed these moments, things, and experiences to occur. I allowed the same types of influencers to support my smallness rather than my energetic bigness. Until I name it, I cannot truly claim the healing, the rebirthing, or the joy of being the real me.

Some of you who are reading this are no doubt already starting to argue your position. That's wonderful—it indicates that you are getting to a new place. Be gentle with yourself. You may protest, "I did not allow my parents to treat me so cruelly growing up!" Perhaps not, but you have allowed the repetitive story to play over and over in your life as an adult. You have allowed people in other relationships to treat you in similar ways. The brilliance of our Creator who lies within us is that until we go deep inside ourselves and really process these truths, we will not benefit from the greatest mystery of cocreating our world. We cannot get the blessings of being a cocreator until we truly own the cocreation of our painful lessons and sorrows. We cannot say we cocreate with Spirit, God, or the Creator while we are blaming God every time we have a bad day.

If you get a divorce, it is important to be willing to dare to get to a place where you can appreciate the gifts of the marriage rather than thinking only about the draining energy and trials of it. The ultimate goal, for the real you to come through, is to get to a complete space of celebration and appreciation while knowing that the energy of "I allowed" must be firmly in place as you're getting there. We do not want to keep repeating the same patterns, but until we name each pattern and claim it, we will bring new people, careers, and experiences into our lives that just produce the same results.

The same idea holds true for moving away from your family. Until you change the energy within yourself and connect to the roles you have played in the family system, you will see that a geographical change heals very little.

Let's look at the word *family*. As we move through life, we discover that *familiar* is a very powerful word. We tend to be drawn to new experiences, yet they feel familiar to us. Such an experience is initially welcome. We will say things like "I feel comfortable with him. There's something about him that I really resonate with, like a piece of my old favorite luggage." The root of *familiar* is *familiaris*, the Latin word for family or household. Yet our eyes also need to see the ending of this word, "-liar," which has its own specific English meaning in the Temple Hayes dictionary of life. When we repeat the same patterns over and over again with new people, we have made a liar out of ourselves in affirming we were seeking different. We have given up our seat.

A few years ago, I started realizing that I was repeating some of the same patterns with people. The people were different initially, but the result was always the same. I started writing in my journal, using the word *familiar* and being very honest with myself about the person and situation I was experiencing. There were two common themes in each situation: (1) I was there, (2) I allowed it.

This variation of the Serenity Prayer can help us through such a situation: "God grant me the serenity to accept the people I cannot change, the courage to change the one I can, and the wisdom to know that one is me."

If you look at the beginning of the word *familiar*, you see that it is "famili-." Thus, we are often attracted to the ways of our past, the things we long to outgrow. The people in our lives change, but the results do not. We feel comfortable and at ease. Yet then there is the back of the word, "-liar." We are often drawn to parts of our lives that feel good at first, yet we come to realize that they are part of our past and not part of our future. We no longer fit in the scenario.

This is a very important teaching on how we want to change yet stay the same, especially in close relationships such as partnerships or marriages. After the newness wears off and we are no longer on our best behavior, we need to be willing to understand how "we allow" and continue to project the same patterns of our past onto current and future events, or we will never shift.

The strongest influence we have, which often evokes dread rather than stimulating immense learning, is our past.

I like to compare the experience of life and its many paths to traveling in an automobile. There is a reason that the rearview mirror is so small compared to the windshield, which we look through to move forward. There is some great wisdom in the fact that our past should be smaller than our present and our future. I always seemed to recognize this, and this knowledge supported me in becoming a great athlete, for I could forget about the bad play or the wrong move. I could also let go of a grudge in a relationship, for it was easy to understand not to carry it over into a new day. I seemed to know that the new day involved looking forward through the large windshield rather than staring in the rearview mirror at where I had already traveled.

Can you let your rearview mirror reflect the past as a smaller path and embrace the grand vision of the windshield of your future journey?

Can you see that you made some choices that kept you from being the real you, such as drinking? Or smoking or taking drugs? Or settling? Or playing small? Or blaming rather than claiming? Or becoming your parents rather than finding them in your becoming? Can you see the influencers that continue to be of the past rather than experiencing yourself as the main influencer of the present and the future?

Can you see, through your windshield, you taking care of yourself, accepting responsibility for yourself, and bringing the new you into the current moment?

Can you let your rearview mirror reflect that you failed at your former marriage but have learned what not to do next time? Can you see, through your windshield, the real you meeting another real person who wants to dance and laugh with you all the days of your life?

If we continue to see ourselves in our past, we will continue to repeat our past in our current and future lives.

My love of life has become a true passion for me. Who knew that someone who almost killed herself from so many automobile accidents while under the influence, who went to jail twice, would end up being a life activist who reminds people every day, "Be the real you and don't take your life for granted"? Miracles are truly possible. I am a living miracle, and so are you. Bring on the miracles and the magic.

I believe that we are born with this amazing energy by the very nature of our being, and when we die we are supposed to have as much energy as, if not more than, we were born with. This belief, unfortunately, is not supported by most people. The influencers try to teach us what to think rather than how to think for ourselves. They teach us that every event in our lives must take more and more of ourselves away. We are taught that by the time we are a certain age, we will be very old and will have less energy and vitality. We are taught by some of our communities that we will die around the same age as our parents or other family members. We are taught in some environments that by the time we are forty or fifty we will be tired and old and that it is too late to dream, create, or thrive. You can see on every television channel at any given time promotions for what you need to do to avoid a heart attack, the medication you need to take to be energized or less depressed, and how to replace hair or take it away. It is one thing to be proactive and make wonderful choices in our lives that will support our youthful energy and vitality; it is another when we are coming from the energy of "giving up our seat" of being the real us.

It is not proactive to take precautions to avoid something. There is a cocreative law of life that is always working, even for the people who say it is not working; it works for them by not working. When you come from an energy of "I have to do this to avoid that," you usually bring the "that" to you. Heal the sensation of the "that," and your belief will support the truths of your discovery.

Nor is it proactive to stop daring to raise the bar to be more than we have ever been before—to accept the ordinary as our ideal.

Anytime we take action based on a choice of avoiding or not wanting something to happen, we are bringing the lower vibration of what we do not want to happen into our creativity. We are a culture that avoids the idea of death so much that we do not understand that because of this avoidance of dying, many of us never live. Dying is natural; not living is not.

How You Celebrate Your Birthday Is How You Celebrate Your Life

How do you celebrate your birthday? Your birthday is the most perfect day, week, or month to reflect on where you are in your life, where you would like to be by your next birthday, and all the ways you are grateful for the life you have been given. *Do not let age be your cage.*

Acceptance of your age is essential to staying vibrant and energetic. People often state that they feel disconnected from their Creator or disenchanted with their lives, and they do not see how disowning their age and the gift of life keeps this negative inertia of separation active.

When we shy away from celebrating our birth in this amazing life, are we not saying to our Creator, "I am no longer comfortable celebrating my life as I know it"? Are we not saying, "I am not comfortable in my human suit anymore at this age and at this time"? And then we wonder why we are not inspired, connected, energetic beings with a life force that is beyond measure. We wonder why our creative juices stop flowing. We are the ones who stop living and stop giving.

Excitement about your life includes embracing the age you are and all that you have walked through, kind and unkind, along life's journey. Our age is one of those areas beyond our control. The only thing we can control is how we accept our age and the willingness to not resign ourselves to the belief that we will have the same outcome as others. Aging is very unique and original. Look at the amazing lives of role models such as Betty White and Barbara Hale (aka Della Street). These women are in their nineties and are thriving with life.

Aging is inevitable, whereas growing old is optional. Growing old is a belief and a condition foisted on us by people who have been the most negative and least insightful influencers of our lives. The fear of being old generates trillions of dollars in our society as we long to avoid how we are designed. An ageless spirit spends quality time researching what is appropriate for the body, what is best suited for a long and healthy life. We have tremendous potential when we celebrate the real me. We can have an amazing youthful life if we do not surrender to the influencers, such as advertisements, or ways of the past, such as how our parents aged or were old before their time.

People, especially women, will often not tell their age—the actual number of years they have lived—because of the way others prejudge the energy and well-being of a person based on that number. The other day I was having lunch with someone who told me that "John is actually an old man now." And I said, "How old is John?" since I knew the person telling me was in her mideighties. She said, "He must be almost a hundred by now." One of the reasons I moved to Florida, where so many elderly people come to live after they have retired, was to leave behind the culture in which people start talking about how old they are when they are in their forties.

With all our modern knowledge, why do we not double our current life expectancy? Like the four-minute mile, which no one could conceive of before Roger Bannister ran it, why do we not raise our consciousness and our bar and aim to live beyond 100?

I am aiming for 150—why not? Certainly no one will be upset if I fall short of this dream. When I say this, everyone in the audience has a good laugh—but remember how everyone laughed about the new idea of airplanes or going to the moon. All great ideas that stretch our current paradigm cause people to laugh and make fun. I would much prefer that someone laugh and make fun of me because I aimed too high than because I aimed too low.

We know more, yet we often are not showing more. Most people who talk about aging simply approach it from the fear of a worst-case scenario. Most people say, "Oh no, I don't want to live to be old and unhealthy and drooling on myself" rather than "I want to break the record as the longest living being on the planet who is still vibrant, energized, and totally connected."

I was old by the time I was twenty because I was weary. I felt so disconnected and misunderstood by everyone around me, and I could not understand why I was born at the wrong time in humanity. You feel old, no matter what your age, when you are weary and scared that no one will ever truly see you. Most significant, you feel old when you have never seen the real you.

Events do not age us. The lack of our participation as our true selves in the events is what ages us. Remember to sing "Happy birthday, real me." Celebrate your life, and in return, your life will celebrate you.

Four Bones You Need in Your Life

Someone wise once said, "Always keep these four bones in your life":

1. **Backbone.** You will always need your courage. It takes a courageous person to let go, let live, let God, and release control. It takes tremendous courage to be who you are and live without hesitation, judgment, or self-imposed limitations. We truly accept our life path when we accept that all the events, people, and places we have experienced have been necessary to make us who we are. This knowledge is the highest surrender to trusting in our life path. We are in the now. In shamanism, the past, present, and future are one time. There is no time in Spirit; the only time is now. *Now* is infinite, with unlimited potential.

2. **Wishbone.** You will always need to keep your dreams in your heart. Our dreams are waiting on us to come true. It is crucial that we continue to greet each day with wonder and awe about our lives and know that in the present moment, all things are possible. Life occurs in the now. Dreams are the stretch marks that continue to birth us into our authentic selves.

3. **Funny bone.** This is an essential ingredient, since we tend in adulthood to take life so seriously. Watch funny movies, and laugh to yourself when you make a mistake. Laughter multiplies once you start it, and it is one of the main ingredients for staying young. Remember that fun, energy, and love all go where they are desired. Improve your now moment, this very moment, by embracing joy.

4. **Hollow bone.** Always leave room every day for the mystery of life to flow to you. There are so many new moments in life wanting to be realized by way of our own consciousness.

Somewhere between the "used to be" and the "can be" is a space of possibilities. Your slate is clean each day—what mark are you going to leave on it today? Make your metaphorical markers erasable ones rather than permanent ones, knowing that a brand-new day welcomes a brand-new you. Living in the new moment is so powerful.

This folk wisdom has frequently been an anchor for me when I have gone through the storms of life and feel challenged to be the real me. These insights help me remain forever young, shining as a lighthouse rather than jumping into a rocky boat.

Don't Forget How to Row Your Boat

Do you feel weary from time to time? Are you beginning to feel old or perhaps tired of the same old stuff day after day? Take a moment and sing "Row, Row, Row Your Boat," and your energy will immediately shift. Childhood songs keep us young at heart and in body.

I have spoken at an AA retreat for the past ten years, and each time the facilitator asked me to tell the people in attendance how to row their own boats. It's so fun for me to lead a group in singing "Row, Row, Row Your Boat." At first it is evident that many people have become a little too rigid and conditioned to let go enough to enjoy singing. Usually, more than half the room will hold back and not want to sing. They may think they are going to get by with not smiling and not letting themselves go, but I stay the course, and soon they realize that we are going to do it over and over until everyone gets fully into it.

We really did have all the wisdom we needed as children, and this song is one more reminder of how this is so. Take a moment to sing it:

Row, row, row your boat
Gently down the stream
Merrily, merrily, merrily, merrily,
Life is but a dream.

The song says to row *your* boat, not someone else's. Many people dedicate most of their lives to trying to change others. The irony of this is that the people they seek to change don't want to change. They are stuck in their positions, and if they were ready to change, they would do it themselves.

If I tell someone how he needs to change, then he is not making the connection with the change. If he is telling me how he is going to change, then change has already begun to occur. We are not here to play God; we are here to show people how God can work in our lives so we can play. It is not our job or place to seek to change others. We are to set an example, and if others desire to change, it will be organic. More important, because they make the choice to change, the change will be everlasting. They have learned to fish rather than having you feed them fish.

If someone changes because of you and it is not truly an embodied change, one of two things will occur: She will abandon the change and go back to her old ways, or she will abandon you. Usually it is the latter.

If you attempt to row your boat with your oars but your oars are in someone else's boat, what will happen? You will be going in circles. When you take your oars and use them to move someone else's boat along—your boat will go in circles. (I personally, along with others, have had this experience.) Whenever you feel like you are going in circles, get into nature and take a time-out, for it usually means you are trying to run someone else's life in addition to your own.

Buildings don't move, and zebra stripes don't change, so please allow others to discover truth by the way you live rather than by your attempt to act out a determined hero archetype of fixing and changing them.

The other side of the issue is when someone is trying to row your boat. We are surrounded by commentators and unsolicited coaches who want to tell us how to be and how to do. You can easily and lovingly tell them to row their own boats.

Thank heavens I ultimately did not believe my sixth-grade teacher when she told my parents I was never going to amount to anything because I talk too much, and thank goodness I knew enough not to believe my friends when they told me they did not think I had a drinking problem. (They had one, too.) And thank God I did not believe most people when they told me that gay people would never be accepted by family, friends, or anyone else.

These are a few examples of how people are not usually accurate when they're telling others how they need to live. If I had listened to these comments, I would most likely not even be alive to write this book.

We need to row our boats "gently," as the song says. Gentle caring for ourselves is a challenge. It means understanding the difference between "I made a mistake" and "I am a mistake." It is the subtle difference between being rigid and being lighthearted. A gentle spirit knows how to go with the flow most of the time rather than trying to push a sailboat when there is no wind.

The effort it took for me to not criticize myself and mentally beat myself up will surely go on record as being one of my greatest breakthroughs. I would consistently attract friends and lovers who always started out being very loving, but then over time they would turn into the critical parent. Why was I was still doing this to myself?

People will always treat you as you treat yourself. If you criticize yourself, others will criticize you. If you dismiss yourself, others will dismiss you. If you let yourself be last in line, others will let you be last in line. If you give up your seat, others will take your seat. If you say mean and rude things to yourself, then others will talk the same way to you. This is especially true of your children. They will grow up to be a miniature version of you—mini-yous in a minivan. Scary thought, right?

As the real you unfolds, make a decision to no longer beat yourself up for any reason. There have been studies in which people have repeatedly yelled at trees, and guess what? The trees died. Japanese author and entrepreneur Masaru Emoto has shown that speaking to water angrily changes the way it appears under a microscope. Since humans are more than 90 percent water, wouldn't this same simple principle apply to us and our well-being?

We will not be free until we free ourselves of the anger, the judgment, and the mean spirit we carry inside our being. We take the energy of separation and turn it into being angry at our Creator, when all along we are the ones who have disconnected.

"Down the stream" is another wonderful clue from the song about how to live. It is certainly advisable to go with the stream of traffic on the highway; otherwise we would experience one accident after another. When we are going against the flow of our lives, we feel as if we are participating in one subtle accident after another. We cannot push the river upstream. I am sure you have heard the saying, "Don't make things happen; allow them to happen." Allow life and its adventures to come to you.

Remember: What you are seeking is the real you.

A couple of years ago, I went to Abadiania, Brazil, to see the world-renowned healer John of God. I wanted to have the experience of being in an area where millions of people had come in the past fifty years. Throughout my ten-day stay, I realized how many dogs had been abandoned on the street and were nearly starving. Yet people who were dressed all in white to visit the Casa de Dom Inácio de Loyola just passed these dogs by every day.

I could not be blind to the lack of humanity and spirituality of this. Even though the abandonment and mistreatment of animals is a global issue, I never expected to see such neglect occurring in the midst of miracles; the dichotomy was too extreme. I will always be grateful for the teaching I received in Abadiania that highlighted for me the extreme dichotomy that is either evident or lying dormant within each of us—not only in a town in Brazil, but in cities and cultures everywhere. We want all the benefits from our Creator, yet we continue to separate ourselves from the other things our Creator created.

I was walking through the Casa grounds one day, and a dog ran up to me, crying, and jumped into my arms. We changed each other's lives that day. Later we named her Sofi.

I promised several of the dogs that I would bring them back to the United States and find them homes here. My friend Carol Gruendl and I made arrangements for the dogs to be brought back. A couple of veterinarians, Turene Frazao Parente Jr. and his wife, Fatima, helped us to decide which dogs would be best suited for the trip.

One of the dogs was named Scruffie, and Carol and I both said, "Will a dog named Scruffie be easy to adopt?" So Carol suggested Lola. Lola was adopted right away by a beautiful family. It was as if she knew that the two women were to be her parents because she immediately ran across the yard to greet them. After a couple of months, I said to one of Lola's parents, "You know, I don't normally believe in changing an animal's name. However, her name has been Lola for only a short time. If you want to change her name, I am sure she wouldn't mind." Her new mom said to me, "Last year, I told my students that I had a dog named Duke and that one day I was going to adopt another dog and name her Lola."

These are the everyday miracles that occur to us, through us, and all around us when we are going "down the stream." Life is so incredible that you just can't make this stuff up. Sofi started all this when she found me in a crowd, and now I run a nonprofit organization called the Sofi Project. Sofi lives happily and joyfully in her prosperous and healthy life in Seattle, Washington. One dog has changed thousands of lives, just from one act of going down the stream and my willingness to say yes.

When we are rowing our boats gently down the stream, we can be in the space of "merrily, merrily." Where has the merrily part gone? I noticed at my twentieth-year high school reunion that most of my classmates were talking about being married and having children or being unmarried and/or never having children. Many of them were talking about their businesses, how many homes they owned, or where they have traveled. Not one person talked about whether he or she was happy.

I remember asking a friend of mine about being happy, and he said, "What does *happy* have to do with anything?" It has everything to do with not dying a little. Happiness is a true measure of whether one is dying or needing to be reborn. When I am not expressing the real me, I am not tapping into the joy of being happy. I am not truly living life merrily. I know a number of people in my generation who attempted to live a life as a heterosexual and at the core of their soul could not be happy that way.

I have known many people who are married and are so dedicated to the idea of marriage that they miss the "happy" part; they are two people who not only have grown old together but have also made each other old.

As children, we are in awe of every moment. We have so many unique expressions on our faces as we look forward to the next moment. As we get older and become adults, however, we start to have a very serious look on our faces, and we start to lose all our joyful and exhilarated facial expressions.

We forget so quickly how life is equal to the attitudes we show to others. Imagine what your place of work would be like if you walked in on a Monday morning and told everyone there how excited you were to see them, how over the weekend you had looked forward to connecting with them again—rather than spending most of Monday and your employer's money talking about how you would rather be somewhere else.

I was a corporate employee only a few times as an adult. The last time was in my forties, and I could not believe how people in a Monday-to-Friday job spend most of Monday talking about the weekend they had and most of Friday talking about the weekend to come. What a waste of time, energy, and resources when being present could offer so much value to the organization and the individuals. We may think we are cheating our employers, yet ultimately we are cheating ourselves, and we will pay a price in some other way.

We are designed to be in awe of our lives.

Finally, the song tells us that "life is but a dream." Your dreams are waiting on you—the real you—to come true.

I waited the first half of my life for my dreams to come true, and many of them did; however, I lived long enough to discover that the true secret of a happy life is to understand that life is but my own dream of becoming the real me.

Have you ever lain down for a short nap in the afternoon, and you wake up and it is dark? You are somewhat startled, for you have no idea how long you have been in such a deep sleep. This is the way life can be if you are not living in the question and answer of happy birthday, real me. You will find that you are waking up and being involved in a life you do not truly fit into.

The New Testament tells us that new wine will not fit in old wine skins: "No one sews a patch of unshrunk cloth on an old garment; otherwise the patch pulls away from it, the new from the old, and a worse tear results. No one puts new wine into old wineskins; otherwise the wine will burst the skins, and the wine is lost and the skins as well; but one puts new wine into fresh wineskins" (Matthew 9:16–17).

The real you is longing to emerge. It is crucial to allow some parts of yourself to die in order that the true you may live. Don't continue to live like a beggar at the gate.

The Beggar at the Gate

There's a story about a beggar who shows up at the gate of a king's palace. At the entrance to the palace, there's a sign that says there is going to be a big celebration and that only people who are wearing royal robes can attend. The beggar looks at the sign and looks at his rags, and a voice within him tells him, *Why don't you try to go?* So he knocks on the gate, and when the attendant comes, the beggar says, "Sir, I need to talk to the king. I want to come to the banquet."

The attendant goes and consults the king, then comes back to the gate and brings the beggar to the king. He looks at the king and says, "Sire, I would love to come to the banquet but I don't have any clothes." And the king looked at him with such compassion and said, "Well, I'm glad you came to see me today. Because I'm going to take you in and introduce you to my son." So he takes the beggar in and introduces him to his son, and his son brings him into his room and picks this beautiful wardrobe, this beautiful outfit for the beggar. And the beggar puts it on and goes to the mirror, and he's basking and identifying with that look and how it feels to be so prosperous.

And over there in the corner he sees his rags, and the son, the prince said, "You know, you won't need those anymore because these clothes that you have of royalty, they will last you forever." And the beggar looks at him, but he reaches down and he grabs his rags, and he puts them in a bag, and he carries them throughout the evening with him. While he's sitting at his meal, he's holding them right there in his lap, kind of distracting but he holds them. And everywhere he goes for the rest of his life, he's carrying these bags of rags. And people talk about him, and he's known as the man who carries his bags of rags.

And that's an interesting story when you think about it because I think that's true for all of us as human beings, in this process that we call spiritual unfoldment, that we have this outfit, we have our spiritual consciousness, we have a Creator that provides us with everything we need to do, anything we want. It's our inherent nature. It's the God within us, a gift of the kingdom, yet we still hold on to the rags of our past, the rags of limitation, or the rags of criticism and perfectionism that keep us in bondage. Sometimes we still even wear our rags, being afraid to change into the new clothes. Do you relate to that?

When I was in my twenties and thirties, I often sabotaged my life and became broken emotionally, and thus financially, so my dad could save me. I would create situations from which I needed to be rescued. Even though I was a great demonstrator of miracles (new riches), I would go home to my dad like a sad puppy (in my old rags) crying for help. When I look back on that now, I see that on some level I was longing to have the childhood I never had with him. I also think I wanted him to "pay" for the things he had done to me.

One day I shifted and became clear that I am an eagle, and I never had to wear or even carry those old rags again.

We can be determined to carry our old rags around in places where we feel broken and not allow the new, emerging, real self to come through. We can be determined to stay stuck in our positions and reject the new riches.

I have owned Yorkshire terriers (Yorkies) for almost twenty years—I love the breed and the dogs' personalities, and they are just so cute. For the past eleven years, until recently, I had two litter mates who were brothers. During the writing of this book, both died.

For many years I said I will always have Yorkies. Recently, because of work with the Sofi Project and animal rescue, a woman contacted me about a Papinese she had named Misfit. He was a seventeen-pound, one-and-a-half-year-old dog, and the woman could no longer keep him because she had a brain injury. I went to pick up the dog, and she kept telling me that I was really going to love this dog. I said to her, "I need you to know that I am not going to be keeping this dog for myself. However, I assure you I will find him a new home."

On the way home, my friend who had accompanied me said, "You are not going to let this beautiful dog go, are you? He is like a dog in the movies—so smart, attentive, and full of life." And so I brought him home, and with his brilliance, presence of life, and big brown eyes, he is now a member of my family. I had to change his name to Mystic rather than Misfit, however.

Mystic has helped me more than I can say with his fun and loving presence, always wanting to play. He helps me grieve for my other dogs and the loss I have felt. He brings a greater sense of life into our home.

Yet I would have denied myself this gift because I had predetermined what my future was going to be (to have only a certain breed of dog). I would have missed the opportunity of these riches that Mystic has given me.

Take a look at your life in terms of old rags and new riches. Perhaps you are returning to certain financial challenges or a predetermined opinion that denies you something wonderful. Perhaps you will not give up an addiction when a new relationship or spiritual awareness is urging you to change your life.

It is time that all of us consider, as we cocreate the mystery of the divine, letting go of the bag of rags that we have been toting around, knowing that we are royalty and knowing that we are divine.

How Deep Is Your Love?

When we resist the divine path of life before us, we experience pain and struggle, and our energy becomes disconnected and drained.

I was always so much deeper than the rest of my family. Do you relate to that? I used to say to my mom when I was a teenager, "Why am I so deep?" And she'd reply, "What are you asking me that for? Let's go back to the football game." But I'd persist, saying, "Mom, why am I so different? Why do I have to be the one who's different?" And she'd always say, "You know what, Temple? I don't know why. But I can tell you that if you'd stop fighting it, it will all work out, because God has a plan for you."

That truth has stayed with me all my life. And I'm sure that you relate to it, too, because we all are different. It's in our spiritual nature to be different. But when we fight it, when we try to hang on to the rags of the past—when we say, "Oh no, I'm not ready for that step. Oh yes, I know I need to move, I know relocating is what I need to do, but I'm just not willing"—and we keep resisting it or we just begrudge it, then we're letting go of our authentic selves; we're not bringing in our true divine birthright. Whatever the move or shift that you need to make for yourself, be willing to let the Creator guide you. "Not my will but Thy will be done."

Not the old me but the new me. Not old rags but a new robe.

Happy birthday, real me!

Ideas to Process and Integrate

～⌘～

Celebrate a tremendous sense of freedom of the real you by being able to dance and feel and sing while claiming your "seat" in life and being unwilling to give it up.

In what area of your life are you giving up your "seat" and being unwilling to give up? In what area of your life are you "giving up your seat" right now?

In order to be a thriving tree, it is essential for us to honor the value of pruning ourselves from time to time.

What people, places, or things do you need to prune out of your life?

Beware the influencers! When we surrender to what others say even though it does not feel inherently right for us, we give up the seat of the real me.

Who are your influencers currently, and how are you being affected by them?

If we continue to see ourselves in our past, we will continue to repeat our past in our current and future lives.

Do you have areas of your life that feel fami-liar?

How you celebrate your birthday is how you celebrate your life.

Define how you celebrate your birthday.

Which of the four bones do you need to strengthen in your day-to-day life?

When we were children, we were in awe of every moment. We forget so quickly how all of our lives is equal to the attitudes we show and see in others.

We are designed to be in awe of our lives.

The real you is longing to emerge. It is crucial to allow some parts of you to die in order that the true you may live.

Don't continue a life like that of the beggar at the gate.

Take time to look at your life—the old rags and the new riches.

❦ 5 ❦

Oh, the Places You'll Go—It's You?

Step Five: How to Take the True You into Your Relationships

How and when did we lose our intimacy with our beloved Creator, with one another, and with all living things, but most important, with ourselves?

How did we evolve by not evolving, to forget that we are born of this earth and that therefore all of creation is truly one?

How do we begin to be reborn in order to remember this quest of life we are so fortunate to be part of?

Perhaps the word *intimacy* itself is the first place we could use more insight, more respect, or maybe some deeper reverence. Perhaps you have seen the word intimacy before explained this way. The word *intimacy* translates into "into me see"— a simple way to identify with our relationship to life. Many people are longing to grow up, understand life's meaning, perhaps aching to release addictions, not really wanting to die while they are living, and feeling drained and disconnected. Yet there is always going to be one truth common to all: we all long to be loved, valued, and respected.

Those who are deeply wounded often pretend it isn't so, yet at everyone's eleventh hour—and I have witnessed many eleventh hours—everyone wants to be loved, valued, and respected. At the end of our physical lives, we all want to grab hold of something greater than ourselves, either through last-minute desperation or inspiration. It doesn't matter what credentials you hold, how much money you have, or how many boundaries you succeeded in setting with your children and others. At the end of your life, you are at the mercy of the inner you and how much you are loved, valued, and respected. So why are we not able to be in touch with this while we are living? And how do we expect to live a truly vibrant life if we have disconnected ourselves from all of life's main sources, especially that which created us?

Thomas Merton once said, "There is in all visible things . . . a hidden wholeness." I would add that the fundamental root of wholeness is knowing that one is loved. We have been so influenced by information and data that have made us robotic rather than utilizing our innate connections. We have believed that we are separate from our source, separate from our planet, and, most important, separate from one another. As long as we believe that we are separate from all these, we will always sense that something is missing. It is the something missing within each of us that the influencers have been aiming at. It is this feeling of "something is missing, I have a hole and need to fill it" that keeps us vulnerable to spending, buying, charging, using, and being delusional. The deeper missing element continues to create a longing to be fixed rather than a celebration and a space in which to come from wholeness.

In other words, we must move from the *hole* to the *whole*.

Can you see it? As long as you feel something is missing, then you will buy "the solution" that is touted as being able to make the missing feeling go away. It is not natural for us to have this missing feeling, since we were made by the Creator to be infinite, to be whole, and to lack nothing.

We will buy almost anything to not feel like we are missing something, when all the while what we are missing is ourselves. We are coming from the premise that we are broken and need something different from who we are, when in fact being different is who we are.

You yourself are the eternal energy which appears as the universe.
You didn't come into this world,
you came out of it like a wave from an ocean.

—Alan Watts

As Alan Watts reminds us, we are born of this infinite earth filled with energy, possibilities, and the highest dreams imaginable. How then can we be drained, tired, and perpetually discouraged? The main reason is that we are attempting to live a lie of our true inheritance. We are like the beggar at the banquet in the previous chapter, determined to carry around our old rags.

We All Desire Love

All living things desire love. Plants do better when we talk to them. Wild animals settle into a new rhythm with an animal communicator because they feel heard, and thus valued and loved. Addicts discover the value of life, as I did many years ago, because someone at the core of our being said, "You are loved and you are valued."

Diseases of various kinds can often be transformed when love is at the forefront of the solutions. Louise Hay and Elizabeth Kübler-Ross were able to prove this decades ago with the rise of AIDS victims. Louise Hay changed many adult lives, and Elizabeth Kübler-Ross proved that babies who were HIV-positive were healed when treated with love and nurtured.

Intimacy ("into me see") is truly where all of life begins: with the inception of love. A planet that loves us gives us the gift of life, and we have this life in all of its joys and complexities until we return to the earth as ashes and dust.

I love the story of the Jewish man who carries a sheet of paper in each of his two pockets. On the sheet in one pocket he has written, "I am the cocreator of my universe," and on the sheet in the other pocket he has written, "I am but ashes and dust." This is a beautiful way to put life in all its paradoxes into perspective. It keeps us alive, awake, and alert, understanding the value we bring to our own lives as cocreators yet humbling us to realize that at the end of this life we are all just ashes and dust.

The ashes-and-dust story is an old one, however, and has often been used to grind people into dust before their time. It is for us to remember that the dust is really stardust and that one of our tasks on this planet is to find the balance between ego and victimhood.

Remember, even a doormat cannot serve its purpose unless someone has written "welcome" on it. If you do not welcome victimhood into your inner home, it will find its way elsewhere.

It is for us to discover on this journey what deep down we have known all along: who we are being and what we are becoming.

Yet it is sad that many people continue to repeat everything; they continue to have the same everything that they say they no longer want.

To Love Oneself

There is a lot of energy and judgment against a person who loves who he or she is. So many traditional teachings have repeatedly told us, "Love us, love our beliefs by forgetting yours; love us as your leaders and follow our rules, and abandon yourself. It is wrong to love yourself. It is too selfish." Yet the traditional teaching, "Love your neighbor as yourself," clearly implies that we should love ourselves.

Actually, the truth is the opposite, because a person who doesn't feel it is okay to love who he or she is will spend a lifetime being selfish and insecure. "See me, see me, see me" comes from an inner lack of being able to see oneself. People who do not love themselves are self-obsessed and not self-actualized. People who love who they are, and who welcome all the newness they encounter on this relationship of discovery with themselves, know that they have more of themselves to give away. It is a pleasure to give this love away. We never run out, for you cannot run out of the natural love that our Creator has blessed us with.

We have been taught by self-made teachings of controlling personalities that it is wrong to have self-esteem and wrong to have a strong ego, when in fact the opposite is true.

A few years ago, I was interviewed on Lifetime Television by the host of *The Balancing Act*, who asked me, "How do you describe self-esteem? Is it nature or nurture?" I said "It is nature. We are all born with self-esteem; otherwise a baby would never ask for food when it was hungry. We all have self-esteem, yet if we are not around people who have it, we tend to stop using our esteem muscle, and we become passive-aggressive and insecure." Some of us were fortunate to meet people along the way who were mature and balanced and who nurtured us back to the self-esteem we had started with. Many are not as fortunate, and they spend their lives craving to be recognized and validated by others for gifts they have failed to express all along.

When you have self-esteem, you are clear that it comes from nature. It is your life gift, and it has your name on it. If you have never had it and are ready to begin to nurture yourself, you will embark on a new journey.

Nature blesses us with self-esteem, and nurturing enables it to grow.

What We Name, We Claim

A number of years ago, I realized that my life had been guided by a simple, self-ordained "PHD": *P* is for prayer, which is breathing in and out every moment of our lives. *H* is the element of humility, and *D* is for devotion to who we are and where we come from. We are naming all the things in our lives, and we are further claiming them with our affirmations, declarations, and conversations. We are always naming the things we are giving energy to and thus creating them over and over.

Prayer: Breathing the Breath of God—The P of PHD

Each time we breathe the breath of God, we are praying into that which is infinite, and our lives have the potential of claiming the infinite by allowing it to be so. We can stop saying, "Oh, how beautiful, it took my breath away," and declare for ourselves that all of nature's beauty is "breathgiving" rather than breathtaking.

In the beginning, the biblical book of Genesis tells us, God created the heavens and the earth. The first humans gave all living things a name, and we have been naming things ever since. We name things *good, bad, right, wrong, ugly, joyful, pleasant, awful, magnificent,* and *miraculous.*

As you explore this concept, you will see an old adage take form: Small people talk about other people. Ordinary people talk about ordinary events. Great people talk about great things.

Observe in your life the people who talk about great things, for they have a lot of great things to celebrate and talk about. It does not mean that they do not have problems or challenges from time to time, but out of despair they will create many more great moments. They will also rally to any occasion and will not die that often while they are living.

Some great thinkers have said, "Don't let your good be the enemy of your best or your ordinary take away from your extraordinary. Don't lower your standards and settle for far less that you can achieve. It is one thing to have a good relationship and perhaps another to say, I have the best relationship beyond my wildest dreams. I love the idea of us being born and reborn by the idea of stretching. We begin our lives with someone being willing to stretch so we can arrive, and our lives require us to stretch further into who we are becoming. If nature thinks enough of us to stretch so we can be born, let us think enough of ourselves so we may stretch into what nature can make us.

A few years ago I started a radio show called *Moving from Good to Amazing*. I loved the show because we were offering tools rather than rules through which people could move beyond a good life to an amazing life. It seems that the marketing and public relations did not carry the message as far as I would have liked, however. I was advised that perhaps my approach was *too* positive and more than the average person could grasp—that most people are trying to figure out how to get through the day or the week and aren't really seeking to be amazing. If so, that's sad. So I changed the name of the show, and in my own inner quest I began to see how seldom people use big, miraculous words.

Most people give their energy to small words. Everyday language has become one-liners like "How are you doing?" with answers like "Not too bad" or "Well, I have been worse, but compared to everyone else I should be thankful." You know you're in trouble, however, when someone replies, "Why do you ask?" Yikes! These questions are actually meant to provoke a point rather than prove one. What happened to "Every day is an absolute miracle! Things are going stupendously! I have more miracles than I can count—it just gets more and more amazing!"

I started to take notice how my energy and vitality increased simply because my vocabulary started to grow larger than my experiences of the moment. So my prayers of affirmation and declaration started to shift, which began to expand my day-to-day world in a greater and dynamic way. The more I became excited about the mystery of every day the more I love the mysteries that came to me during the day.

I wrote a song a few years ago for my beloved partner, BB. She is a cancer thriver. Notice I didn't say *survivor*. She created the term *thriver* to add life to her state of being. That's obvious, isn't it?

Although I wrote the song for her, as I thought about her journey, I thought of so many other people in my life whom I have known and loved and observed walking through tremendous experiences as a human being, facing their challenges in new and dynamic ways.

Here are the lyrics to my song, "It Is Amazing":

> It is amazing.
> It is amazing, when I look across at you
> and I see what you've been through.
> How did you do it?
> Walk the miles through all the rain
> as you felt shadowed with your pain.
> It was amazing.

To watch the lights turn on in you
when you said "Yes" then God came through.
Oh, how you've touched me.
As I've watched you through the years
create the smiles where there were tears,
you see, you told me.
How I've often changed your life
as you've had challenges and strife,
and yet I tell you,
watching you has taught me how
God can work right here and now.
It is amazing.
It is amazing.
When my heart can feel such grace
and home is more than just a place,
It is my blessing.
As I look across at you
I see God come shining through.
It is amazing.
Loving you has changed me so,
seeing you've I've come to know
God's grace is amazing.
God's grace is amazing.

So life, for me, is to be amazing, not simply "I'm doing pretty good." Or "I'm getting by."

We are missing the opportunity that comes with prayer. It is not something we do several times a week; it's the thoughts and feelings we hold in our hearts. When we are praying, we are not going to our Creator and speaking some unknown request; when we pray, we are saying, "Yes, I hear the desire within me, and I am willing to follow it through to its completion. Show me the way, and I will take one step at a time toward this new way of becoming."

Humility: Creating an Open Heart—The H of PHD

Humility is the second element of our PHD. When we pray (or call in) what we would like to be our next experience—whether it be a love relationship, a healing, a new teacher, or a new friend—there must also be an agreement with our Creator that we will be open to what this experience might look like. Packages of *yes* can come in all shapes and sizes.

After I prayed for a healing in my late thirties because I was drained and disconnected and needing help, I never dreamed that I would end up for many years on the floor of my shaman teacher's den going into otherworld realities to discover the true me that had been so influenced and lost by the wrong GPS navigation.

Before reaching such a deep level of desperation, I would never have been drawn to my teacher because she was tough. I had been so busy climbing the false ladder of success that I never stopped to ask, *Is this what success really means to me?* Berenice held nothing back. She was candid and sometimes hard. My personality wanted to walk away at times, but the High-way of me, my soul (the Higher way of Spirit), knew I had to stay. I knew in my humility that she was the one for me. I would have probably passed by her many times in a crowd because of her silent way of being.

When we first started our work together, she would laugh at me and would call me on my stuff. I wasn't used to that. I had surrounded myself with a whole village of people who hung on to every word I said. They even took notes, and here she was telling me I knew very little about spirituality. Now, by the time I met her, I had been considered a leader at three spiritual communities. She wasn't saying I was not filled with Spirit (we are all spiritual); she was saying I had been exercising surface spirituality with my head rather than integrating the true deepening of spirituality within my heart. She was tough on me and still is.

Yet she is the one who came to me, and I knew she was right for me. I needed to be open to receive her gifts even though they were in a different package from what I thought I wanted and needed. She was blunt and stubborn, just as I am, and a profound and brilliant librarian. She was a teacher who, like so many teachers before her, was not swayed or influenced by how much she loved me. She was the one, and my soul knew it. Humility is the ability to see and hear from an open-spirit perspective what we have brought into our lives because we at some point have prayed it into being.

When I sent for the dogs in Brazil to be delivered to the United States, I was surprised to see that a four-year-old dachshund had made the trip. The dog had been saved from cancer, and the Brazilian vet did not feel comfortable giving him to just anyone, so he sent the dog here, knowing he would perhaps have a better life.

This precious dog ended up temporarily living at my house with seven other animals already coexisting with my family. We welcomed this little guy with open arms and at the same time put great energy forth to find his perfect home. I named him Chico Man. He was a true winner in every way. Names are very important to me, so during his one-month stay at my house, I was surprised when I would call him Buddy. Then I would say to Chico, "Why do I keep calling you Buddy when your name is Chico?" And he would just smile at me and wag his tail.

A friend of mine said she had given a photo of Chico to a friend of hers, who would call me. A couple of weeks went by, and then he called. He asked me many good questions about the dog and seemed very interested to meet him and possibly make him a new addition in his life. Toward the end of our conversation he said to me, "I am looking for my buddy to share my life with." Wow—that did it for me. I had the humility to see and hear that this was a God-dog job and that the connection had been made.

Chico, aka Buddy, went to live with Wally, who was in deep grief. He had lost his wife, who had left him, and he did not want to live at any high vibrational level. He had pretty much decided to go to his job a few hours a week, make enough to play a good game of golf from time to time, and then lie on the couch the rest of the time and feel sorry for himself.

Chico was attempting to bring Wally the healing he needed, for Chico had been given a second chance. As a cancer survivor, he was ready to truly live, and Wally was not being open and engaged within his own humility. He didn't want to have to walk a dog three or four times a day. This dog had come into his life to help him learn to stop dying and start living again, but Wally was too blind to see it. He called me on more than one occasion and asked me to come and get the dog, but I would always take my time, for I knew that the two of them had great work to do together. The last time Wally called, I asked BB to go and get the dog, for he deserved so much better than this "I love you, I can't love you" scenario.

Fortunately for all of us, BB was running late on the day she was to get Chico. When she got Wally on the phone, he said, "I am so thrilled you are running behind schedule. This morning Chico kissed me on the face. It's the first time he ever did this, and I realize how much I love this dog. I can never part with him, for he has given me my life back."

Wally had prayed for help, and God had given him the love and healing packaged in Chico Man, yet he had to have the humility to trust the process and let the change come into his heart. Wally and Chico can currently be seen on the golf course, at the barber shop where Wally works, and wherever the two may go; they are always together. What a love story! Both guys were healed of their insecurities and their disbelief in surrendering to love. Both guys were given a second chance to truly live. Oh, the places you will go if you allow it!

Robe Washer

In my early forties, I went on a sacred shamanic journey, seeking to know more about myself and what awareness I needed to experience so I could be a more balanced spiritual being. As I entered this deep meditation, I was met by several people, and they took me up on a small hill. They reached over to the side where we were standing and placed upon me an incredible gorgeous red and gold robe. It looked like something Elizabeth Taylor would have been proud to wear. It was so elegant and warm. I took to it immediately—I have always had the type of taste that desired the finest of things. So this beautiful, elegant robe got my full attention. I could feel it and be in it as if it were a real experience.

In a moment or two, the individuals removed the robe and put it away. They were taking it away from me. One of them grabbed me by the hand and then walked me down to the river, where there was a woman washing robes. The robes were all sizes and shapes, all were white, and some were torn. The woman was scrubbing them and placing them into a large cauldron. Then she hung them on a line to dry. She said to me, "Robe Washer!"

When I returned from the meditation, I spent time writing about this vision. I realized that I was more than wealthy, for I was connected to the infinite resources of the earth that had birthed me, yet in order to truly experience the depths of my spirituality, I needed to keep my ego in check by knowing part of my nature as Robe Washer. No matter where I may go in my life, what my credentials are, or how many people are interested in what I have to say, I am Robe Washer. I am never too good or, I hope, too arrogant to ask for forgiveness or to allow people to be who they are. I do not ever want to be a know-it-all, just a robe washer who knows nothing at all; therefore, I can know everything and anything. I am humble to what can be rather than determined that things have to be.

Just saying the name Robe Washer brings me from my expression of presumed arrogance to sacred humility within seconds. I am able to shape-shift from self-righteousness to self-right thinking in a matter of seconds.

Humility is not a word of weakness; it is a word of great strength. Humility makes the space between *what used to be* and *what can be* a space of gratitude. Humility is the immense energy that reminds us how fortunate we are to be birthed on this planet and what a privilege it is to know we are never separated from Mother Earth and Father Sky. We are all one woven fabric of the divine.

The Classes of the Spiritual Path

Another way we can lose our ability to be humble is when you aim to have more, compete, and be more than anyone else. Often we drain our energy when we compare ourselves to other people and assume they have a much easier life than our own. For years, we have had influencers remind us of the value and sense of accomplishment of being upper class. We prejudge that the upper class has it made. Economically we categorize people as upper class, middle class, and lower class. I would like to dare to identify a spiritual "class system" as well. The *upper class* is made up of people who are enlightened, awake, making a difference, and participating in a new era on our planet. They are usually as introverted as they are extroverted. They do not need to be known for the sake of being known, yet to share their message beyond a few hundred individuals, they must be known across the globe. These people can manifest material wealth yet not be changed by it. Their value is not measured by how much they own or have. They understand that the package we die with is either a box or an urn, and neither holds many things. The upper class is here to help remind all living things of the value of cocreation and collaboration. These people are what we call old souls. The upper class is here to keep our vibration raised so we can keep living people alive so they do not die an early death while still walking on Earth. The upper class do not allow the conditions of the world according to the news to make them weary.

The *lower class* consists of people who are regular attendees at a traditional house of worship and who know more clichés and scriptural quotes than most of humanity. They are the talkers with very few walkers. What they say is not congruent with what they do. They have accepted being a lower vibration as the new norm. Their mantra is "What difference does it make? We are going to die anyway" rather than "I could make a difference if I would stop being part of the walking dead."

The *middle class* is made up of people who are somewhere between the upper class and the lower class because they want to straddle the fence and please the other two classes. They have not surrendered to and immersed themselves in the upper class because they are too afraid of what people will say—their team, their congregation, or their family. Middle-class people try to stay in the middle, never having a voice and rarely being heard. Rather than being influencers, they are people influenced by the following:

- Needing to be liked
- Being current with the biased news
- Not speaking up

- Being passive-aggressive
- Playing God instead of allowing God to play through them
- Singing other people's songs but never writing their own
- Rowing other people's boats rather than their own

Middle-class people never get to experience what being upper class would mean for them: detachment, the tremendous satisfaction of being self-actualized, and empowered. They would be able to see change resulting from a few authentic ripples in the ocean if they were simply willing to take a few more steps into courage. Middle-class consciousness could also change the way the lower class perceives the world, because the middle class can relate to the lower class better than the upper class can. Middle-class people could greatly shift the way the lower class just gets by and barely lives, but the middle-class people won't speak up because they need to be liked too much to take the risks involved in being a change agent.

The middle and lower classes have always been rich, but they rarely know it. They dwell on what is wrong and needs to be fixed rather than celebrating what is working and going well. They believe that they are being "done unto" and that they are given more than they can handle instead of seeing that they are the ones who are choosing what they handle.

The lower class is filled with the sleepy and the weepy. These people feel sorry for themselves and perceive that the principles of life do not work for them, while actually the principles are working for them by *not* working. They are influenced by everything and everyone else. They not only waste their own lives, they also usually have little to no respect for other living things.

We have much to do and be on this planet and with each other.

It is possible for an individual to move into each of the classes from time to time. I have lived them all, and I understand how we can go from one to the other. My goal is for you to see that the true upper, middle, and lower classes of our society are not necessarily the economic ones. Spiritual class is defined not by how much money you have but by how you use your spiritual riches and let go of the old rags. Spiritual wealth celebrates equality and delights in people coming together to eliminate some of the world's chronic problems. When we have the eyes to see more clearly, we become united rather than separated.

Each of us has been given an incredible divine inheritance. All we need to do is to wake up and stop dying a little every day so we may master our own lives.

Poet Ella Wheeler Wilcox expressed this sentiment well in her poem "Which One Are You?":

> There are just two kinds of people on earth today,
> Just two kinds of people, no more, I say.
> Not the rich and the poor, for to count a man's wealth
> You must first know the state of his conscience and health.
> Not the humble and proud, for, in life's little span,
> Who puts on airs is not counted a man.
> Not the happy and sad, for the swift counting years
> Bring each man his laughter and each man his tears.
> No, the two kinds of people on earth I mean
> Are the people who lift and the people who lean.
> Wherever you go you will find the world's masses
> Are always divided in just these two classes.
> And oddly enough you will find, too, I mean,
> There's only one lifter to twenty who lean.
> In which class are you?
> Are you easing the load
> Of overtaxed lifters who toil down the road?

Or are you a leaner who lets others bear
Your portion of labor and worry and care?

Leaners are disconnected and drained, whereas lifters are impassioned and energized.

Devotion: Dedication and the Divine—The D in PHD

Devotion is the third element of our PHD. Individuals are impassioned and energized in their lives when they are devoted to the belief that life is a unique gift.

We are like little cups of God; we are here not to play God but to allow God to play through us. God is inside us, and until we cease to resist owning this as our reality, we will always feel drained and disconnected rather than impassioned and energized. Although many years I was living the lower vibration in the lower class, the upper-class part of me recognized itself as true and bold and brave. I began to start moving out of being part of the walking dead and began to return to the roots of my understanding as a mystic and spiritual being. I began to shed the layers of misinformation and to remember the God I was devoted to in my childhood, which helped me to survive being spiritually and sexually invalidated. I began to wake up.

Many people spend their entire lives being devoted to their families of origin, their teachers of influence, or things they don't want rather than ever stopping to say, "Who am I? Can these ideas be true and real? Where am I determined to be headed without using my own head? Am I a lifter or a leaner?"

Scripture gives us an opportunity to step into the higher vibration of being upper class: "While Jesus was still talking to the crowd, his mother and brothers stood outside, wanting to speak to him.

Someone told him, 'Your mother and brothers are standing outside, wanting to speak to you.' He replied to him, 'Who is my mother, and who are my brothers?' Pointing to his disciples, he said, 'Here are my mother and my brothers. For whoever does the will of my Father in heaven is my brother and sister and mother'" (Matthew 12:46–50).

As an avatar and a shaman, Jesus understood that there are a few major roles for us to understand in order to allow God to play through us:

1. We are whole made in the image and likeness of God.
2. We are therefore infinite.
3. We are related to our own families, yet more important, we are related to the Creator who gave us life.

As we surrender with our own inner PHD (prayer, humility, and devotion), we understand it is one thing to get along with the family, yet this can limit us in understanding our greater inheritance if we are unable to allow ourselves to emerge into the planetary family for which we are destined. We are here to come from wholeness, infinity, and interconnectedness. Our families of origin are valuable in helping us see what we want to be and what we don't want to be, yet it is our Creator and the energy of creation that brings us into our true being.

When you really look into where you're going and where you are, you will understand that all of life is connected and measured by how you think, feel about, and know yourself.

If you do not love yourself, then you do not believe your Creator can love you. If you do not respect yourself, then you do not believe that the laws of life can respect your affirmative prayers and actions. If you do not relate to all your blessings, your gifts, and all the special parts of your personality, then you will never believe that others or God will relate to you, either.

I am always stunned when I hear people in recovery talk about how angry they are at God. What they are really saying is how angry they are with themselves. Leave God out of it. Actually, this is what got them in the mess in the first place: they left God out of it. Their innate and intuitive God talents told them from the beginning, Don't go there, don't drink, and don't smoke. But they did it anyway, and now they blame God. I love the following statement: God can get you the garage, but you have to drive your car into it.

God gets blamed for so many things that have nothing whatsoever to do with God. This I know, for I did it myself for many years. In certain situations, when we are unable to say, "I allowed this," we appear to be losing common sense. We must first and foremost accept that our relationship with ourselves is equally an expression of how life will be with everything else—not some things, but everything.

Many orators and motivational speakers and some popular ministers tell us repeatedly that God wants us to have everything and to be happy and fulfilled, and although this sells a lot of DVDs and books, it is only partly true. God cannot give us what we are not able to see and accept. We will not see it; we will pass it by, sabotage it, and ill-wish it.

Until we are ready to accept that we can be happy and fulfilled, impassioned and energized, we will not believe that there is a God who wishes it so. I know this to be true from all the years of being a scientific study myself.

The Relationships That Free or Bind Us

I once heard someone say, "If the world is round, why take sides?" This statement has stayed with me for the past thirty years, for it is profoundly true.

We especially create sides concerning men and women. We are determined to make the sexes so different, so unique, and often at odds with each other. We learn techniques, styles, and ways of communicating with the opposite sex so we can ultimately be heard and feel connected. We have more information than we have ever had, yet we still have a divorce rate of more than 50 percent. Don't you think this is odd?

People are attempting to have a relationship with someone else when they do not even have a relationship with themselves. When heterosexual women discover that I am in a very healthy and long-lasting relationship with a wonderful woman, they often say to me, "Well, perhaps I ought to try the other side and see how that goes." However, the difference is not whether you are with a man or a woman; the difference is how you are with yourself. How you are with yourself will always be the deciding factor in how someone else relates to you. The sex and shape of the person will not change that.

You can love a man or a woman, and the intimacy, personal dynamics, and interactions will be the same depending on whether you have ever changed. In my life I have actually been a trisexual. I have tried both sides, and even though the physical shape was different, the external relationship was the same until my self-love and acceptance evolved to a different level. When I changed on the inside, my love relationship changed on the outside. When I discovered intimacy with myself, my partner was there to be the mirror as well. We should encourage ourselves and one another to embrace both our feminine and our masculine aspects, with respect for both the divine masculine and the divine feminine. We are all carrying the yin-yang energies of creation within us.

A friend of mine was once finishing a project for me, and she said, "Men—who needs them!" I said, "Please don't say that—actually *you* do. Within you is the masculine, and you cannot abandon an entire part of yourself." We are all masculine and feminine. It is not because we are both that we have challenges and misunderstanding, it is our denial of one or the other that creates the hardships, challenges, and differences.

Many years ago, I was in a gay relationship with a much older woman, and we went to a bar in Savannah, Georgia, while on vacation. There were very few places you could go back then if you wanted to live to tell the story. A man came up to us after we had finished a dance and said, "Which one of you is the boss?" I said to him, "We don't work together, we love each other." We love each other, therefore we are equal.

Nature does not say to us, I give you light and dark, but one is the boss. Or I give you the inhalation and the other exhalation, but you decide which one gets to call the breath.

As I told my friend, please don't separate yourself from the masculinity you have within you. It was a defining moment for me, for I realized how far I had come.

Oh, the places I had been in my life: almost attacked as a child on two separate occasions by men, having a raging dad and an alcoholic grandfather, and having no luck whatsoever with men as lovers—both guys I had a crush on told me they were gay. Boys were afraid of me in school because I was brave and tough and such a good athlete. I did not "get" men. I did not understand them, and most of the ones I let in abandoned me and caused me deep pain.

Now here I am, all these chapters of my life later, as an advocate for men. Change is always possible if we allow ourselves to go to new places. Men deserve better than what they are getting now.

In my thirties and forties, I had a very supportive and loving relationship with a man named Jack and then a long-term relationship with a lovely, wonderful woman named Marla before I met my forever life mate, BB. Both of these earlier relationships were able to offer me as much as I could offer me. They could give me only the depth of love that I was able to allow within myself.

We all teach others how we want to be treated, and I was able to offer only so much to Jack and Marla because I was not evolved enough at the time. I would often pretend, people-please, or feel uncomfortable taking a stand for myself. I was coming from middle-class spiritual awareness: I would not say what I felt or ask for what I needed. I was acting as though my lovers were psychic and they should simply know in advance what I always needed. I also had to grow out of the old idea that relationships are hard, for I had watched my parents live in this paradigm the entire time they were together. They had to work hard at pretending they were happy and had to work hard to make things work.

We have been told so many times in the fairy tale about Snow White that we owe, we owe, so off to work we go. We often believe that in order to have a fairy-tale romance we must work hard to get it. We somehow believe that knowing it is hard will enable us to succeed at it.

I am so grateful that I never gave workshops on finding your soul mate or how to succeed in love relationships, because I would have said trite things like you have to make sacrifices, opposites attract, get used to it and make it interesting, or it's just hard work and one compromise after another.

That was before I became an upper-class person.

I was making sacrifices in my former relationships, with both a woman and a man, for I was sacrificing the true me. I was not showing up as totally true, so how could I have been seen as totally true? I was always told that opposites attract, so I would think that a lot of opposition was just part of a relationship. When your values are so opposite to someone else's, how can there be true joy in the relationship? I thought compromising was what was necessary to be happy in a true relationship, so I was not honoring the promises I had made to myself. So many people today are continually compromising who they are because someone told them that this is natural. It is never natural to sacrifice who you are and at the same time expect to be happy. Nor is it natural to be unhappy long-term.

As a spiritual leader, I see this all the time. Partners get together to avoid being lonely, and they settle time and again—either seeking to stop the desperation or longing for some inspiration to come from outside themselves.

A woman once said to me, "I am looking for a man who is into spiritual practices, who will want to come to church with me, who will enjoy being with my children, and who will benefit from loving my animals."

The next time I saw her, I asked how it was going, and she was glad to share: she had met the love of her life and was going to run away with him. "Tell me about him," I said. She told me that he is an atheist who doesn't like children and is allergic to animals!

She ran away from herself long before she began to dream of running away with him. She is not awake. She is dying and is too blind to see it. How long will her sacrifices last? I wonder. I am sure they won't last too long, since these qualities of his are totally out of alignment with the woman and her inner calling.

After all the false pretenses, partners are actually surprised when they do not make it. Common sense is one of our most precious God ordained gifts.

When will we understand the difference between being alone and being lonely? Being alone is about developing our inner sanctuary and establishing a true relationship with who we are and are becoming. Loneliness does not stem from the absence of another person; it comes from the absence of you—your true self.

As a teenager I had a poster in my room that said the following: *I am often more lonely in the midst of a crowd than I am by myself on a mountaintop.*

Loneliness is a state of being wherever you are, with however many people you are with, when you are not being the true you.

From Soul Ache to a Full Heart

While I was in my relationships with Jack and Marla over a seventeen-year period (and also on separate occasions), I had a soul ache, for I was longing for more than what I was getting. Yet it wasn't their fault or shortcomings; I was wanting more than I was bringing. However, I was getting back just what I was bringing. That's when I had an "aha" moment, the realization that I wasn't putting my whole self in. I realized that what I believed spiritually and how I practiced as a learned shaman were not being reflected in the current flow of my life. I was still bringing my past beliefs from my family system to the relationships. I was still toting my old rags to the banquet of my new life.

I was somewhere between the lower class and the middle class while wanting to fully express in the upper class. Yet how could I do it? I was so programmed to believe old worn-out ideas about love.

I started looking into the mirror and singing to myself the song from Firefall: "You are the woman that I always dreamed of / I knew it from the start / I saw your face and that's the last I've seen of my heart."

At that time I was employed at First Unity in St. Petersburg, Florida. I noticed several times how the minister, Alan Rowbotham, looked at his wife, Kathryn, and those moments changed my life. It was a look that Hollywood has mastered on camera but that very few people I have known in real life have had. It was the look that said, "I honor you, I adore you, I respect you, and I admire you."

Watching them in those moments, I remembered a scene when I was fifteen and sitting in the den of my grandparents' home. My grandmother Rubye was in the kitchen, and she yelled to my grandfather, "Howard, what are you doing?" He said, "I am sitting here looking at Temple Ann." He was looking at me intensely, as if to say, "I honor you, I adore you, I respect you, and I admire you."

That memory had been lying dormant in me, and seeing Alan and Kathryn look at each other woke me up. When I was able to put the look into words, I was immensely sad and definitively glad at the same time.

I was happy that such a look existed but sad that I had had it only one time in life, with my grandfather. I knew that as long as I continued to hold myself a certain way and live in a certain manner that I would be loved. I would have a good life, but I would never truly be honored with such grace.

I finally got it. I got real with myself and connected with the deeper belief that everyone ought to have the look like those two had. Everyone ought to be honored, adored, respected, and admired, and it could easily be reciprocated.

So my prayer to call the look into my life began, and the rest, as they say, is history.

You cannot get what you do not bring. Oh, the places you will go! You will take you to the banquet of life. Be what you want to see; allow yourself to receive yourself as whole, infinite, and more than you have yet to imagine, and it will be so.

Ideas to Process and Integrate

Into-me-see. Take time to explore the word intimacy and the relationship you have with yourself. Make a list of what you want yet do not have and ask yourself, "Is this what I am bringing to my experiences?"

One common truth, no matter what anyone ever tells you, is that we all want to be loved, valued, and respected.

In what ways do you love, value, and respect yourself?

Make a list of the main relationships in your life, whether they are at home, at work, or in community. How do love, value, and respect manifest?

As long as you feel something is missing, then you will buy the "solution" so the missing feeling will go away. We will buy almost anything in order to not feel like we are missing out, when all the while we are missing out on ourselves.

What do you feel is currently missing in your life? Who would you be if you had it?

We will always have one common thread on our journey: who we are being and what we are becoming. Those who continue to repeat everything will have the same everything they say they no longer want.

Do you have any repetitive patterns in your life? If so, what are they? Where did these patterns begin, and what actions or awareness will make them cease being?

A lot of judgment is directed against a person who loves who he or she is: "It is wrong to love yourself. It is too selfish."

Describe moments you have felt "selfish." Is self-esteem nature or nurture? I say it is nature. We are all born with self-esteem. Self-esteem is your life gift, and it has your name on it. Nature blesses us with self-esteem, and nurturing allows it to grow.

How does self-esteem manifest itself in your life?

Small people talk about other people. Ordinary people talk about ordinary events. Great people talk about great things.

What do you talk about?

Leaners are disconnected and drained, whereas lifters are impassioned and energized.

Are you a lifter or a leaner?

When you really look into where you're going and where you are, you will understand that all of life is connected and measured by how you think about, feel about, and know yourself. Our relationship with ourselves is equally an expression of how life will be with everything.

People are attempting to have a relationship with someone else when they do not have a relationship with themselves.

What matters is not whether you are with a man or a woman but how you are with yourself. How you are with yourself will always be the deciding factor in how someone else relates to you. We are all carrying the yin-yang energies of creation within us.

What attitude of perfectionism, holding back or criticism do you keep repeating in relationships? Are you ready to truly experience the incredible you and have others notice? Begin inside—the places you will go—you will go with *you*.

6

Your Dreams Are Waiting on You to Come True

Step Six: How to Allow Your Dreams to Become Real

One day a teacher asked her first graders, "What do you want to be when you grow up?" and she received several great answers. Julie said, "President of the United States!" Tommy said, "I want to be a major league football coach." John said, "I want to run my own company."

The teacher was waiting to hear what Billy had to say. "Billy, what do you want to be when you grow up?" she prompted him, and he replied, "I want to be possible." She asked what that meant, and Billy explained, "Well, my mom is always saying that I am impossible, so I want to grow up to be possible."

When we are born into this physical existence, we know innately that we are possible. We are connected to the infinity of the universe, and therefore the sky's the limit. So what happens to us? How do we go from dreaming and desiring to dreading and disclaiming? How do we go from joy and wonder to feeling disconnected and drained? How do we go, within the span of a few years, from possible to "that's impossible"? If we are born to innately know we are possible, then what changed to create the belief in being impossible?

The answer is very simple. We have been trained and programmed to believe that it is entirely up to our strong will and determination to make our lives and our dreams happen. We supposedly adopted the ways of our ancestors, yet did we really? Originally the ways of our people before us were more principle-based. Even as recently as 200 years ago, our ancestors were operating from an inner awakening of Spirit that is reflected in these words of the Declaration of Independence: "to assume among the powers of the earth, the separate and equal station to which the Laws of Nature and of Nature's God entitle them." When you really take to an open heart this declaration of being independent, it is amazing how it was just a short window in humanity when it was written. And yet, here we are disconnected and drained, people barely living, many on medication and coping with dread. We have people killing their own, murdering their children, and animals being treated as if they do not have a life that matters at all.

It seems evident that it is time to get back to working with rather than against the Laws of Nature and of Nature's God.

How does a small plant burst through the cement? Through the inner awakening of Spirit.

How does a metal object fly 200 to 300 people all over the world in the sky? Through the inner awakening of Spirit, which expressed itself through the inventor in the belief that an airplane was possible.

How does an alcoholic like me, with more accidents than can be counted on my fingers and toes, walk away from the addiction and never look back? Through the inner awakening of Spirit, which was allowed to become possible within me.

How does a wild animal become tame? Through the inner awakening of Spirit.

How does someone walking around half or mostly dead in every way but physical begin to thrive again? Through the inner awakening of Spirit.

The Importance of Inner Approval

We are innately gifted with what we need to be possible and for our dreams to come true, yet we have been programmed to seek outer approval rather than inner approval.

So many new concepts promote the idea that you must find yourself on the inside rather than seeking yourself from the outside. Those who are impacted by teachings of scripture would relate to this statement, Romans 12:2: "And do not be conformed to this world, but be transformed by the renewing of your mind, in order to prove by you what is good and pleasing and perfect will of God." In other words "Be ye in the world but not of the world." This is a great axiom, but what does it actually mean, and how can it benefit us to live as the inner awakening of Spirit? Bumper sticker clichés are great for a car, or a magnet on a refrigerator, yet unless we integrate them into our being and understand why they need to have depth and meaning, they are somewhat useless.

Here are some qualities you need to live from the inside out rather than the outside in:

- Clear knowledge that all is well even though appearances may indicate otherwise.

- Time spent in nature every day.

- The ability to connect the dots with each phase of a daily journey: the name you thought of, the phone call that came in, the person who invited you to a meeting, the book that fell off the shelf.

- The belief that other people's opinions of you are not that important— you are long past the teacher's report card.

- The ability to be so present in the moment that, for example, when you are sharing something with someone on the phone that maybe you ought to have kept to yourself and the call drops off, you realize that perhaps it was meant to be rather than a "coincidence." Or your computer goes blank just at the moment you were going to send the email to someone even though you were hesitant about it in the first place.

- The ability to celebrate delays rather than being angry and denying them.

- The understanding that your exes are not the reason your life doesn't work—they are your sacred friends who made the real you begin to work.

- The realization that no one has ever been against you—even the most difficult people in your life shaped your path.

- Clarity that people's views of you have very little to do with you and more to do with themselves.

- An embrace of what spirituality in the presence of your enemies truly means.

- The understanding that the people who could not "get" you created the space for you in which you had to "get" yourself.

- Acceptance that your addiction was not wasted living but that it helped you survive the false you, which was wasting the real you.

- The realization that the world is not black and white, it's both. It's *both/and* meaning it's black, it's white, and it could be a different realization all together.

Mystery Perfected by Design

A number of years ago, I was driving down the highway with a little girl who was about five at the time. She would always get philosophical with me because she knew I was capable of allowing her to do so. She was in the backseat talking away, and she said to me, "Life is weird, and it just doesn't make any sense. It's crazy!" She added, "We are born naked and then we die naked. I don't understand it!"

I immediately responded, "I feel the same way—it is crazy and it doesn't make that much sense to me, either, but maybe that's by design. Maybe we need to not understand it so we will go deeper within ourselves to seek to understand it."

She was pondering a sacred thought that many of us have had, and she was right: It *is* pretty weird and crazy unless you know, embrace, and embody the purpose of the space that lies between the nakedness.

Perhaps life is perfectly designed to be a mystery so we can allow the mystery to be perfect by design. Deep, right? But think about it: The mystery is a mystery for a reason. I remember talking to a student who was asking me why he could not know in advance that his prayer was being answered. He wanted a peek or a glance.

I said to him, "Let's say you want to be blissfully happy, and you pray today for that to be. Then the next day you receive an overnight package in the mail with a letter that states the following: 'Joe, your prayer has been heard, and in order for you to be blissfully happy, here are your orders. You must:

Relocate to Florida.
Lose fifty-five pounds within eight months.
Let go of those fourteen friends who are intimidated by you.
Quit your job.
Grow up—you are sixty-five.

Leave your marriage of pretense.

Tell the truth for once and stop lying to yourself.' "

This is simply too much at once for Joe to integrate. He needs the mystery of not knowing, and so do the rest of us. We welcome the word *change* as a naked baby and then resist the word for the rest of our lives—at least, some of us do. Our dreams and prayers are answered in the way that is best suited for our consciousness. For dreams and new desires to be lasting and possible, it is necessary for us to grow into them.

Clothed with an Amazing Destiny

How perfect it is that we are born naked and vulnerable so that we may learn how to be properly clothed. The *clothing* of our lives is not meant in a literal sense, although we are required as human beings to be clothed according to our culture, environment, and standards. I am talking about the clothing of who we are meant to be. The clothing we discover in our lives is the core value we accept of our uniqueness and magnificence, and anything less will give us the feeling of being drained and disconnected.

A closet filled with clothes from the past as well as the clothes of the future feels stuffed, weighed down like the beggar who had new beautiful clothes yet still carried his old rags around.

If you are already in a phase of doubting that the life you desire is possible, then volunteer to help a teacher in a kindergarten, work a week in a summer camp, or spend other quality time with little kids and ask them, "What do you want to be when you grow up?"

The answers will be pretty awesome: a famous dancer, the president, a schoolteacher, a princess, a leader who can end hunger, and so many more. Within every child is the desire to be clothed with an amazing destiny. None of them hesitate as they declare, "This is why I came here." At a young age we believe, "I do not know how it can happen, but I know what I want to happen."

I know my dream can be possible. I know I am possible.

We are told in scripture (and I paraphrase) not to worry about what we drink or eat or what clothes we shall wear, for if God takes care of the birds, are we any less?

I have the good fortune of living in Florida, and never once have I witnessed a worn-out egret that affirms how difficult and challenging it is to be itself. There is no struggle, most of all because the egret is not questioning its yesterday today, not holding on to the memory of the fish that someone took away last week, and not questioning why it had to be an egret in the first place. The egret simply is, and all the current energy and vibrancy it has in its now moment is coming from an inner awakening of Spirit, existing in what is and what is possible. The bird is an egret without regret. It is unlimited in being possible.

Old Life, New Life

Perhaps you would say that you do not have any dreams. I would dare to differ. If you continue to live year after year the same way—with the same complaints, limitations, aggravations, and hesitations—then you are living a powerful dream. It is simply a dream in which you stay the same. Do you know how much energy it takes to always keep your life the same? It's exhausting! It actually takes walking-on-water miracles for people to do the same things year after year and get the same results, especially if that habit is to wallow in misery day after day and year after year. It takes a powerful person to wish upon the day something challenging or difficult to happen in order to justify getting a six-pack, a bottle of wine or vodka, or a bottle of pills.

The turning point of experiencing an inner awakening of Spirit occurs when you realize how much energy it takes to not let the true you live. The inner awakening of Spirit actually helps you see what is possible in all the areas of your life where you have died. Once you can start to see that it takes so much determination to keep making your life seem impossible, you can open to what is possible.

Many people in recovery have said to me, "I don't know how to make my dreams come true." I reply, "Well, you have been making your dreams come true for a number of years. The dreams you had were to not feel, to die a little every day, to stay numb and sedated on some level. You had the dream of doing that for years, and you didn't know how you were going to do that, either."

The determination to live your life as an impossible dream proved to you that somehow you could always find a way to get high; someone would always share his or her abundance with you—drinks or drugs—and it would always work out. You were always able to accomplish what you set out to do: to be part of a dream that made you feel less than what you are. You were using the laws of nature to support you in remaining impossible rather than becoming possible.

You often hear reports about people from all walks of life who have overdosed, but do you ever hear of someone who has under-dosed? Hardly ever—why? We are powerful beyond measure, and if we focus on being impossible and staying numb and sedated to life, we can always create a way in which to do so. Now you can even get a prescription and your insurance will pay for it, whereas in my days of being an addict I had to go down roads late at night that did not have a dividing line in the middle and risk my life just to get a drug that would help me NOT feel. Those of you who are determined nowadays to die while you are living have it much easier.

We are working with a set of principles and natural laws in an unnatural way when we are dying to who we are supposed to be.

When you get into the new rhythm of supporting who you long to be instead of accepting what you will never be, you get high every day, but differently. You get high from waiting to see what the mystery around the corner will bring you. You get high by going from impossible to possible. You get a natural high by learning to come true to the magnificent you.

In our society, we have mastered "my way or the High-way" by settling for far less than who we are. We have lost our way in the last seventy-five years, for we have shifted from being principle-based people and are now a consumer-based people. We have lost our way because we are dying from the true meaning and value of life. Just look around you, who's still celebrating? It's time to wake up!

We are often childish, not childlike. We are often not emotional and contemplative but angry instead. Many of us have lost our way from *possible* and have become impossible. Billy was right when he longed to be possible, and you are right as well.

I am reminded of a story about John Lennon, who said his mom told him to always remember that the meaning of life was to be happy. When he went to school and the teacher asked him what he wanted to be when he grew up, he said happy. She told him he did not understand the assignment, and he told her she did not understand the meaning of life. His mother taught him an incredible lesson!

We need to change the meaning of high in "My way or the High-way!" from the high of addiction to the Higher power of Spirit. We must call into our being the inner awakening of Spirit and surrender to allowing our lives to no longer be manipulated and controlled, limited and small, as we open up to a greater plan of what our lives can be.

Once you own the reality that your dreams are waiting on you to come true, you begin to understand that you have had the power to cocreate your reality all along. You have simply been pointing your life down a road that is going backward rather than following the flow of your life forward. You have been going against the grain, and the splinters have been painful.

My way is allowing the Higher-way. This is likened to finishing a prayer or request: this or something better.

A new life cannot be achieved as long as the old life remains front and center. We learn this as athletes. You cannot continue to play the same play over and over and get different results. In other words, you need to dream differently. You are working with the same laws of nature that made you feel impossible; you simply need to dream into your inner awakening of Spirit a new direction to realize you are possible.

Once you start to see that you have always been possible, then all former mistakes are not something you are required to carry like a bag of old rags to every destination. You begin to see how all the experiences of your life have brought you to the High-way, your High-way. You truly have to have a good laugh at yourself when you realize your location on the map of life. You were here all the time. It's like being at an amusement park and looking at the point on the map that reads: *You are here.* Aren't you fascinated that all the parks, no matter where you visit, have the red X painted so small? So you look and look and look and ask someone to help you, and then you realize, *Oh my, it's right here in front of me.*

Once you arrive at your new destination of moving from impossible to possible and allow the inner awakening of Spirit in your life, you can throw your bag of rags away. You can make a different choice rather than being the beggar who toted his old rags with him to every new experience. The difficulty is that most people will want to keep carrying their old bag of rags with them.

I almost killed myself many times from the amount of alcohol I consumed. I was literally committing a slow version of suicide. Yet somehow, by the grace of an inner awakening of Spirit, I survived myself. All those years, I apologized for myself; felt guilt, shame, and disgrace and carried the "I am an accident waiting to happen" energy in my body and my essence. So on the day many years ago when I decided to move from impossible to possible, I did not go down the liquor aisle, Isle 13, in my grocery store anymore.

A beautiful quote by Seneca states, "It is not that things are difficult that people do not dare; it is people do not dare that makes life difficult." My life was difficult for I had stopped daring. I was settling.

I was one of the most successful drinkers I had ever known. I did it well—I gave it all I had at the time. Now I am able to drink water and feel the high. Once the decision was made, my old rags of regret were behind me. I felt so strongly that, because I had already given all those years of my life to being numb, I was not willing to play those stories over and over and be stuck in my misery. I did not wish I could be different; I accepted that I *was* different. I did not wish I could drink, for the best day I had as a partier was never as special as being awake, energized, and impassioned about my life.

People say to me, "Will you be offended if I drink around you?" and I say, "I will be offended if you don't." Think enough of me and give me the credit that, if I could drink, I probably would. But I can't, so why should you try to be like me? Be yourself!

It is beyond my way—it is the High-way of my life. The highest ideal for my life is being free from alcohol, which ultimately means being free from sugar because that's where it starts.

The old rags were no longer necessary. I had seen my life move from impossible to possible. I had witnessed my life move because of the inner awakening of Spirit. I had gone from being a child in elementary school, when my dad made me white toast every morning with lots of butter and white sugar on it, to being a sugar addict, a soda addict, and then a liquid sugar addict of mostly wine and beer.

I had lived long enough from my dying and not living to become one of the healthiest eaters on the planet. Now that is a modern-day miracle.

Yet the key for me was to let go of saying the story all the time. When I drank, I did it well. Beverly Sills, a former famous opera singer, when asked if she missed performing, showed the interviewer her necklace. It had the letters IDTA on it. He looked at her in surprise and inquired, "What is that?" and she replied, "I did that already."

So IDTA, Temple Hayes. I did that already. A new chapter was ahead of me, and I did not need to transfer the addiction to meetings or sad days of dread over and over. I had graduated, and my new of being possible now emerged. I could let the old rags go.

As I said in a previous chapter, we are not here to play God, we are here to allow God to play through us. Being a life advocate means being serious enough to value life yet free enough to experience the joys of life. Many people spend their lives trying to play the part of God or figure out why God is not doing what they think God ought to be doing. People who live in the world of "it is someone else's fault" blame their parents, their upbringing, their teachers, and their God. They are people who have totally been "done unto." They are people who do not let their old rags go.

There's a story of a woman who is having a dream, and in the dream there is a great big green dragon who is chasing her, so she starts to run as fast as she can. The faster she runs, the faster the dragon runs after her. All of a sudden the dragon grabs hold of her, and she screams, "Oh, my God, what are you going to do with me?" The dragon responds, "I don't know, lady—it's *your* dream!"

Your life is your dream, and how you honor and value your life is equivalent to what your life is going to do with you.

It truly is not complicated. We affirm with great passion that we are ready to come true.

Dreams Come True

When I decided to become a public speaker, there were lots of things that had to come true within me. I needed to expand my vocabulary, so I would study word cards while sitting at a traffic light in my car or while waiting on an appointment. I learned how to say "I don't know" and feel comfortable asking people what a word meant when they used it. This is important, because you often learn that someone taught you inaccurately. I had to develop my wardrobe and know what colors were best for me when I was in front of an audience. I took voice lessons so I could project my voice and use my vocal cords properly. I was willing to make lots of mistakes to become a speaker without notes and develop an extemporaneous speaking style. Lots of time, energy, and practice went into this development.

When we see someone who is really good at speaking, writing, singing, or acting, we are so quick to assume that their talent came easily; we neglect to consider all the ways they may have had to come true to become that gifted. We see people who are addiction-free or who seem to "have it together," and we often lose sight of all the journeys, days, and ways in which these individuals have had to come true to be who they are.

You really have to decide if you are ready to come true.

Our dreams are waiting on us to come true. We start where we are by first accepting the law and covenant of life that dreams are meant to come true. There is no question mark. Actually, the challenge in our lives is that we stop living in the question and begin to realize our dreams with a period in its place.

This is part of the great tragedy of the human spirit: when we are little, we all innately know what our dreams are, and we organically are drawn to discovering their ability to come true. The challenge is that children are rarely given the opportunity to validate their dreams.

A few years ago I led a sacred pilgrimage to Peru with thirty-three people. It was an amazing and insightful journey for each of us. When we were on the bus and returning to the airport, I noticed the sadness in one of the women's eyes, and I asked her, "What is so heavy on your heart? Will you miss Peru?"

She told me that she dreaded returning to Florida because she would have to face her ex-husband again, and it was a very difficult relationship. I told her that if she was serious about wanting this relationship to change to give me a call, and I would sit down and talk to her and see what we could do to change the energy that she held for him. A few weeks passed, then she called my office, and we sat down and had a wonderful talk. I was so surprised when she told me that this man had been her "was-bund" (her ex-husband) for about twenty years.

The more she talked, the more I realized that she was the problem and that he was being held captive by her unwillingness to allow him to move on. She was quite shocked when I asked her if she felt selfish for keeping him from moving on with his life and told her that his dreams were waiting on him to come true just as her dreams were waiting on her to come true. As long as she was unwilling to let him go, she was in his way, and why would she want to keep him from having the life he deserved? We did some good work together. I led her through an ancient Celtic shaman technique called *recapitulation*, and we removed the "energy cords" that kept her responding to him as her past self rather than as the person she had become over the years. She was so relieved that she was finally able to set him free and their relationship could take a new form.

She wanted very much to give me something, so one evening she invited me over to her home for dinner. She was a renowned artist, and she had her paintings on every wall. As we were looking at them, I saw a beautiful painting of an older woman holding the hand of a young girl, and they were looking over the beach. I told her that this image seemed so real that I felt like I could walk right into it, and she said to me, "You're going to walk that painting right to your car."

A few days passed, and as I was writing her a thank-you note, I began to sob, for I realized that this painting was a true-life image for me. When I was six years old, my grandmother Rubye brought me from the Carolinas to outside Jacksonville and then to Tampa Bay, Florida, to show me where she was from and to share with me the beauty of the beaches. I had never seen a beach before. It was truly life-altering.

This experience was one of the sacred stories that had been stored in my heart. I always remembered that my grandmother had bought me a beautiful beach ball, but because I did not understand the flow of the ocean and its tides, the beach ball was taken from me by the waves, never to return. That was one of my first experiences as a child of seeing how nature works when you're not working with it. I resonated with a loss and what that felt like.

Four days after I had brought the painting home, I went on a cruise with my family. One morning I was up early and went out on the deck of the ship and started a conversation with a stranger. He was telling me how relieved he was to be relaxing and on vacation. We continued to talk, and somehow we started talking about life, nature, and how people don't seem to understand the innate responsibility of taking care of our planet. He looked at me and pointed to the middle of the ocean and said, "See what I mean? Look out there—someone has thrown trash out in the waters." I was awestruck. I said to him, "That's not trash; that's a beach ball." In the middle of the ocean, decades later, I had found my beach ball within my heart again. After all this time, I was given this experience once again.

I shared this experience with the artist, and she did something to the painting. She added a beautiful beach ball.

These moments of inner awakening to Spirit do not happen just to me, they happen to everyone. As we increase our connection to moving from impossible to possible, the truth will be revealed in our day-to-day reality.

The secret is the willingness to come true. Coming true is not always easy for us to do. We cannot see life in a different way until we are willing to see ourselves in a different way.

It is not always easy for people to allow their old belief systems to die so that their new beliefs can move them from impossible to what is possible. People often become so attached to a story even though the story isn't working. Why would we not be willing to go in a new and different way—a new High-way—if it meant our lives would be changed forever? We can always go back and pick up the old ideas that really didn't bring us much joy in the first place, if we want to. We are natural born cocreators, and as we allow our disbelief to fade away, we bring the new dreams into our lives. We say what, and we allow God to decide how.

Dying is often necessary to birth the new within your being. Allowing old beliefs to die within us is often necessary so we may come true to what is possible.

Dreams are not simply the ideal of getting everything I want or you getting everything you want. Dreams are more an emerging energy that supports our intention of not living with the eyes and heart constantly affirming what we don't want. If we could have everything we ever wanted, we would often live in a world of regret, for often the High-way is so much better than my way. Haven't you ever thought you wanted to be in love with someone, and the universe told you no? Then years later you see the person again, and you cannot believe that you once thought this was the person for you!

We don't want life to give us everything we think we want; we want our soul to recognize what wants us to come true to ourselves. We move from my way to the High-way of our path.

Coming True Through
Shamanic Work

A number of years ago I began to truly feel I had moved from impossible to possible. I was coming true. I had added another dimension to my life, and had begun to do more than work on changing my thinking and my life. I had added the new element of "change your energy and your life will change." I was beginning to experience the inner awakening of Spirit. After years of exploration, expansion, and experiences, I had been given my shaman song. I went on a shamanic sacred journey, and in this meditation I heard a tune with these powerful words: "I am the Spirit of life and the life of Spirit; I am always free. I am the Spirit of Life and the Life of Spirit; the power is in me."

This song was my anchor; it grounded me in walking in the world but not being of the world. I felt invigorated, impassioned, and energized, and for the first time in my life I felt like I could truly fly. I was moving from a chicken to an eagle.

You might wonder how you can get your own shamanic anchoring song. Just as a mother and a father go out of their village to hear the song of their unborn child so they can sing this song for the rest of the child's life, we all have an inner song within us.

First, affirm that you would welcome your shaman song. Second, create the space for you to be in quiet or in solitude. Third, begin to sing the tune or words that come to you.

I made a few attempts before mine finally came, and the day it appeared through me was the day that I believed I would have one and then I let go. Before this particular day, I was trying to force the song, and this did not work. When I received my shaman song, I started using this strong anchor for myself every day. It was a rite of passage I was born to be given.

I learned an immense number of tools for practical application from my shaman teacher. I remember the first time I heard her cast the circle by calling in the four directions. I was spellbound, and my soul recognized the ritual as sacred and soothing to my soul. Like so many things we learn from our teachers along the way, this ritual truly becomes our own when we put ourselves into it. So over the years I added more of me and my thought process to the equation, and this process has helped me live more each day rather than die a little.

I assure you that if you would be willing to adapt this practice into your life, your energy will increase by a noticeable amount. You will change your energy and your life. You will start your day with a great sense of all things being connected rather than of each event and experience working independently of one another.

The Four Directions: A Ritual

I honor the east, whose aspect is *life*. I welcome the birth of life, which reflects new beginnings. I see the new in my life right now. A new beginning is always here if I allow it. I honor air—the element of the east and an element in my body. I honor the winged creatures and thank them for their teachings. I thank them for their ability to remind me every day of the value of "flying over" all the circumstances in my life and seeing them as an overview rather than the only view. I thank them for their ability to show me how beautiful it is to simply be a bird and be it with grace. I honor the spiritual tools of cutting away. I recognize the inner power in my life to release and let go, to cut away energetically the relationships—whether they are people, places, or things—that no longer serve the direction I must go on my soul journey. I honor the spirits and guides of the east. May they be present with me this day and in this circle.

I honor the south, whose aspect is *light*. I welcome the light that I am innately birthed to be. I honor fire—the element of the south and an element in my body. I honor the fire within my solar plexus, the passion of my creativity. I am on fire for my life and am discovering the mystery of being an awakened spirit. I honor the crawling creatures. [When I am leading groups and they are repeating after me, I say this again.] I honor the crawling creatures—yes, each and every one of them. I thank them for their teachings. They teach me and remind me that we must all crawl from time to time in our lives and that we crawled for a long time before we walked.

We often forget that we ever crawled, yet we did when we were little, and we still do. We crawl through various moments of our lives when we endure change, when we lighten our load, or when we move from one phase to the next. We crawl when through death or change we say good-bye to something we love deeply. We crawl when we move from the shadows into the light as we grow out of duality or realize duality is an illusion.

I honor the spiritual tools of balance. May I remember balance as a necessity for everyday application. May I remember not to be against something unless I am for something. May I remember not to disown something unless I own something. May I remember I am woman, yet I am man. I am masculine and I am feminine. May I realize that balance is more than self-scheduling; it is a daily way of living one's life and provides more choices for self-actualization. I honor the spirits and guides from the south. May they be present with me this day and in this circle.

I honor the west, whose aspect is *love*. I honor water—the element of the west and an element in my body. I recognize the value of water in my life. My body is more than 90 percent water. I honor the creatures of the deep. I give thanks for their teaching that I may go to the depth of myself to truly understand what love is and that love can transform all of life's ailments and woes. I honor the spiritual tools of containment. I understand that it is my container that expands or limits my ability to love. How much love can I have? How large am I willing to let the container of my open heart be? I honor the spirits and guides from the west. May they be present with me this day and in this circle.

I honor the north, whose aspect is *law*. I have a deep reverence for a law that is always working even for those who declare it isn't working—it works for them by not working. I honor mother earth—the element of the north and an element in our bodies. I have the wisdom to know that I am not simply born of the earth; I shall also return to her. I honor the four-footed furry creatures; I thank them for their teachings and recognize with sacred attentiveness the value they bring to me. They have brought me many healings in my lifetime, and I await the next one to enfold. I give thanks for the spiritual tools of concealment and revealment. I believe that the truth will reveal itself at the time it is ready to be revealed. I am open with faith that the law of life is a law of growth and that what I am to know and discover shall be. I honor the spirits and guides from the north. May they be present with me this day and in this circle.

* * *

After several months of repeatedly doing this ritual, you will start to notice all the connections and how they work together for your High-way. All these energies, totems, and sacred teachers will change your life by changing you, if you will let them.

As you allow yourself to work with the directions and their meanings, over time you may want to use your own words.

Many people have told me after using this ritual for a period of time how they have more energy and also a deeper appreciation of life. Often people will say they no longer kill insects for the pleasure of doing so when they are not bothering them, and they begin to notice the birds meeting on the electric wires on their nature walk. The more you celebrate being connected to all things; the greater your awareness becomes that you are connected to all things. Life matters and when we treat it as such with everything, we get the benefits of lots of life and vitality in our bodies.

Now that I am sharing with you all my secrets, I wanted to also share with you a philosophy I adopted many years ago: Pay attention to what knocks on your door three times. This has become my way of allowing what I am to know to come into my space.

For example, when I hear or read something and then two other people mention it as well, I know it is mine to do. That is how I became sober, became vegetarian, and got into homeopathy for my pets. Many things have been revealed to me when I have been open to the messages that find me.

Dreams of the Heart

In reference to my dreams waiting on me to come true, I conclude with the greatest and most significant story of my life. Dreams do not always come in the boxes and packages we hope they will or arrive the way we think they are supposed to. Dreams are not limited to this reality, for life is filled with magic and mystery.

Dreams require us to come true to who we are, work from the connections around us, and keep our hearts open. The following story is an incredible example of how I wanted something or someone to be in my life, how I lost her, and how she returned to me in a way I never dreamed possible. She has taught me through her life and her death that nothing is impossible for those who love their Creator and allow the inner awakening of Spirit.

Born deeply philosophical and always questioning life, I longed to relate with another human being who spoke my language. It was like speaking English and going to a non-English-speaking country and longing to meet someone who understood me. I longed to hear someone use the types of words I used, who thought of God as I did, and who related to nature in the way that I knew to be true. Being born a mystic is an immense blessing, but never meeting anyone like you feels like a curse when you are a child.

When I was twenty years old, I met Beverly Alberstadt, and my longing for a mirror ended. She spoke the words I recognized, and she related to God and to others the way I did. It was love at first sight. I adored her! She was the Unity minister in Greenville, South Carolina, and she was thirty years old, so our closeness in age also helped with our connection.

I attended every class she taught, every program she sponsored, and every lecture she gave. During this chapter of my life, I catapulted level upon level to new heights of growth because of all the validation of finally being seen for who I was.

I felt with absolute certainty that she and I would be physically and spiritually connected all our lives. I was therefore shocked when she announced that she was relocating to Alabama to marry the man she had fallen in love with while in ministerial school. Needless to say, I did not want her to go. I had searched for someone like her for fifteen years, and now she was leaving.

We stayed in touch as best you could back then, and one day I called her to discover she was very ill. I had lost my driver's license, and by now I am sure you know why, so I paid friends to drive me to her. I could not believe my eyes when I saw her. She was withering away, and later I discovered she had cancer. She died not long after that, and for years I grieved for what could have been.

I grieved for what I wanted, what I missed about our connection, and I could not heal. She was the second person devoted to God whom I had loved so deeply and who had died young. The memories of losing my cousin Bruce came to life again.

I would share with my therapist, my astrologer, and, from time to time, a psychic the deep loss I felt for her and how I could not heal. I was given processes and journal techniques, among other things, yet with little to no success.

I did not understand how I could have been so clear about our relationship being lifelong when that was not to work out at all. It was indeed one of my deepest disappointments.

One day the inner awakening of Spirit opened up my heart again, and I realized I had to let go. Beverly died in the late 1980s, and a number of years had gone by. She was born on January 11 (1–11), which is important to know.

About five or six years after Beverly died, I was awakened in the middle of the night by my pager going off really loud. For those of you who do not know what a pager it, it is a small box we used to carry around so that people could call us and leave their phone number as a message; then we would find a phone and return the call. My pager went off so loud that it startled me, and when I looked at it, it flashed 111. I went back to sleep, and in a few moments it went off again: 111. I said out loud, "Beverly, is that you?"

The next day, as I left my apartment, there was a huge banner across the street that read BEVERLY'S ANTIQUES—GRAND OPENING. I was having a grand opening, all right! I was on my way to meet with a woman from California; the experience of the last few hours was consuming me, yet I did not feel comfortable sharing it. I asked the universe to give me a sign.

As I was riding with the woman to a restaurant, we decided to have the valet park her car. After he did so, the attendant yelled at her, "Ma'am, I parked your card in parking lot space 111." She looked at him as if he were crazy, and he said it again. Then she looked at me and said she had heard him the first time, but why was he yelling the number instead of just giving her a ticket? I told her that it was actually a sign for me and that I would explain it over lunch. (I still have the ticket all these years later.) When I shared my story with her, she validated it by agreeing that I was getting a visit from someone I had truly loved so deeply.

These encounters have never stopped in my life. I have had these messages through phones and other means of written expression.

I have had psychic readings, and the psychic always hears Beverly giving me messages about my life. She has remained in my life one of my greatest allies, and she is part of my dream. My dream needed me to come true so I could experience the love we had together in a different kind of way—not my way, but the High-way!

Ideas to Process and Integrate

How does a small plant burst through the cement?
Through the inner awakening of spirit.
We are innately gifted with what we need to be
possible and for our dreams to come true, yet we
have been programmed to seek outer approval
rather than inner approval.

What part of you needs to come true so you may be more possible?

Do you know how much energy it takes to always
keep your life the same? It is exhausting!

In what ways do you feel your life is the same? In what ways
are you willing to change it?

We call into our being the inner awakening of Spirit.
We surrender to allowing our lives to no longer be
manipulated and controlled, limited and small, and
we open up to a greater plan of what our lives can be.

What adjustments do you believe are necessary in your own life
for the greater plan to come to you?

A new life cannot be accomplished as long as the
old life remains front and center.
Once you start to see that you have always been
possible, then you do not have to carry all former
mistakes like old rags to every destination. You begin
to see how all the experiences of your life have brought
you to the High-way.

I did not wish I could be different; I accepted that I was different.

The key for me was to let go of saying the story all the time. IDTA (I did that already.)

We often need to let our old rags go. What old rags do you still carry around?

Your life is your dream, and how you honor and value your life is equivalent to what your life is going to do with you.

We affirm with great passion that we are ready to come true. You really have to decide whether you are ready to come true. The secret is the willingness to come true.

Coming true is not always easy for us to do. We cannot see life in a different way until we are willing to see ourselves in a different way. Dying is often necessary in order to birth the new being within you. Allowing old beliefs to die within us is often necessary so we may come true to what is possible.

Dreams are not simply the ideal of getting everything we want. Dreams are a more engaging energy that supports our intention of not living with the eyes and heart of constantly affirming what we don't want.

If we could have everything we ever wanted, we would live in a world of frequent regret, for often the High-way is much better than my way. We don't want life to give us everything we think we want; we want our soul to recognize what wants us to come true to ourselves. We move from my way to the High-way of our path.

Allow yourself the gift of a shaman song. The four directions ritual will energize and impassion you if you are willing to do it several times a week. These energies, totems, and sacred teachers will change your life by changing you, if you let them.

Pay attention to what knocks at your door three times. This has become my way of allowing what I am to know to come into my space.

Name an event or a moment in which this has been true for you. Dreams require us to come true to who we are and work from the connections around us.

7

It's Only a Shadow

Step 7: How to Understand and Transcend the Shadows in Your Life

Have you ever heard the saying "Stop trying to teach the pig to sing—it makes you angry and it annoys the pig"? The longer I live and the more awake I become, the more I realize how challenged we can be at times in accepting reality. Gloria Steinem said, "The truth will set you free. But first it will piss you off."

We find it difficult to embrace and embody the truth—what I am willing to give my life to, the truth that allows me to either live or die a little every day?

As a spiritual leader talking with people for the past twenty-five years, I have discovered that most of life's ailments and challenges come from the inner core of people who are not living their own truth and developing their own individual belief systems. They hold onto facts, limitations, and stories that are not true for them. They do not understand that letting these false truths go will set them free.

Most people are dying a little every day because they are attempting to use an old map that doesn't have the new road on it. It's like someone giving you an old GPS and asking you to use it to find your way to your next destination. It cannot take you to the new place, for it does not have the necessary upgrade.

As you step into the practice of being fully alive, energized, and impassioned, you will receive many natural upgrades in your life. When you listen, observe, and step into these upgrades, you will have immense joy; when you do not, you will experience the struggle of weariness. Many people stopped using their "thinker and soul voice" and adapted to what someone else felt or said, which might be true for one person but not for another. Many people have stopped listening to their heart as their GPS for their heart is closed.

Truth often becomes a litany of blanket statements that are not really accurate. Truth is often debated by people who are arguing over who said what and what it really meant, but very little energy is given to what I say as an individual, and is it true, or what you often say, and is it true.

My friend Tom Costa used to say, "Yea, though I walk through the valley of the shadow of death, I do not have to build a condominium there." We begin to die a little and take away from our energy field when we build condominiums and closed, permanent places in our hearts and minds without even being conscious of it. We become disconnected and drained rather than impassioned and energized.

Shadow Talk

Many books tell us that the power of our words make all the difference in our lives. Our statements determine whether we are energized and impassioned or disenchanted and disconnected. It is crucial for all of us to go through the process of totally aligning with the words we speak and the messages we give and to learn to move beyond the old clichés that often become our way of life. We are using old language with a new emerging self, and it is not impassioned and energizing. We are like the beggar carrying old rags when an upgrade in our words, thoughts, and actions could bring us riches.

Words that are very powerful can become old rags that bind us rather than attracting new riches that would free us. In this section I explore many examples of such untrue statements.

"It's not that big a deal." An individual will describe a situation in his or her life this way. I would ask you to realize that, when people say something and follow it up with this statement, it means they want someone to recognize that it really *is* a big deal. This is a cry for help.

"It doesn't really bother me." This is an easy one. When you follow a challenge, a dilemma, or a circumstance with this statement, guess what? It *does* bother you, and you will become more alive when you learn to tell the truth. We heal any story and transform a painful story into a sacred story when we tell the truth.

"I'll deal with that later." In time management, it is easier to do what you are putting off than to keep repeating in your head that you will do it later. What you put off till later to deal with will often wind up dealing with you. In other words, when I am unwilling to change circumstances, circumstances change me. This applies to the simple to-do list we carry in our heads, the project list we keep at home, and the things we need to do for our children or our friends. We also tote unresolved feelings around with us wherever we go. *Later* doesn't come.

"I can't take one more thing!" Wow, really? If someone wrote you a big check, provided you with an airplane, and treated you to a house in Italy for three months, would you really say this? Of course you can take one more thing. Focus on the one more thing you'd like to take and pray it into existence. The overgeneralizing in your head is

a clear sign that it is your energy that needs the adjustment. Saying "I can't take one more thing" closes off the good as well as the bad, so you are no longer open to what truly belongs in your life.

"Everything happens for a reason." Well, wouldn't you imagine this would be true? It has the inner workings of a very powerful cliché, yet rarely is it used as a complimentary or uplifting statement. Most people use this statement as a nicety or when they can't think of anything else to say—like when someone gets pregnant and she wasn't planning to do so, or when someone loses a job. Sure, everything is happening for a reason, but ultimately that is based on opinion and rarely on spiritual truth. This is often in the "mind file" as a sudden response; it is more defensive than offensive, and it does not allow the person being spoken to an opportunity to truly feel. It's what I call a "metaphysical shutdown."

"I've dealt with my grief; I am doing okay!" When people say this, it is my experience that they are not doing their grief work. One of the leading causes of ailments and deep woundedness is unresolved grief. Gifts await us on the other side of every grief experience, yet because we do not want to feel the pain and we avoid feeling the sadness, we do not get to receive the gifts the experience has in store for us. It is only in the depth of ourselves that the gifts await us. It's like opening a present and throwing the box away only to realize later that there was still something immensely valuable deep down in the bottom of the box.

"Everything that could happen is happening to me right now." Really? This couldn't be true, or you wouldn't be alive to say it. When you make this statement, are you really taking into account all the things that could be happening but are not? Life is not out to get us; it is simply longing for us to "get" ourselves. We are not people being "done unto." You probably are not dying from starvation, so rather than saying that everything is happening, stop and give thanks for

all the wonderful things that are happening (and for all the horrible things that are not). The higher vibration of thanksgiving will cause the wonderful things to multiply.

"What you don't know won't hurt you." Actually, what you don't know can hurt you a lot! Common sense has lost its way, and we need to bring it back to life. We have stopped using our minds and intuitive powers related to our bodies and our well-being. We rely way too much on what other people know rather than asking our inner selves what we know to be true. Here are a few examples:

- The doctor will tell you that you need to have your knee replaced, but it would have helped if someone had told you that if you exceed your natural weight, you will most likely have knee problems.

- Wise teachers have helped me realize that shoes that do not have a strap or a back will cause severe long-term back problems and knee issues because they are not designed to work naturally with the way your body was created. We are not made to shuffle our feet or use the front of our feet to hold our shoes on. Observe how many people you see in public places who are limping or struggling to walk—then check out their shoes.

- Health challenges have to be addressed by working with all of our bodies: spiritual, mental, physical, and emotional. Correcting just one of these areas will only be a temporary fix. An automobile will not run smoothly if you have an engine without the tires or if you have a transmission and are missing the engine. Healthy bodies require the full package.

Life is not one size that fits all. Use your common sense and ask lots of questions of more than one source.

"They are still learning their life lessons." Everything in life is a lesson as long as you can accept that there is not a white-haired judge in the sky or that your worst teacher is following you around with a report card. A lesson would imply that you learn and move on, not that you keep falling into the same hole.

The great Portia Nelson stated the following in *An Autobiography in Five Short Chapters*:

Chapter 1: There is a hole in the sidewalk, and I fall in it.

Chapter 2: There is a hole in the sidewalk, and I fall in it again.

Chapter 3: There is a hole in the sidewalk, I fall in, and I can't believe I did it again. I get out quickly.

Chapter 4: There is a hole in the sidewalk, and I walk around it.

Chapter 5: I take a different street.

"God never gives you more than you can handle." What does this statement really mean? What I have found throughout my years as a spiritual leader and life coach is that most people who use this statement don't sound convincing when they say it. It is yet another statement that people use without realizing that they are negatively influencing people's views of God. In traditional Christianity, we are taught how separate we are from God in the first place, and this has created an energy or a vibration in which many people are disconnected from God. People are often angry because they still live in this reality and think, *How could God do this to me?*

This is where the rubber meets the road. This is where a person either develops into spiritual maturity or remains forever committed to being a victim. We are not all standing in a receiving line for God to give us certain events based on decisions made about who we are. We are not people being "done unto" with a bunch of stuff to deal with.

The belief that God never gives us more than we can handle dismisses the reality that we are participants in our lives. People have a choice of how many children to have. They have a choice of how many things in life to take on and of what to get involved in. This statement robs us of any responsibility. No one in life seems to be spared senseless tragedies; some are evident and can be seen from the outside, whereas others are carried deep inside. When we own what is on our path and look to this path of least resistance, not only will it enlighten us, it will free us.

"That's not my problem." Perhaps we could say this before we learned better. A butterfly flapping its wings in Australia affects us. If something is happening to you, it is happening to me. I learned this when I was younger and a very good softball player. Softball was the vehicle of expression that kept me impassioned and energized. Yet if the other eight players were not any good, I wasn't going anywhere, no matter how fabulously I played. My immense talents meant nothing without the team to go with me. What other people do on our planet is our problem. How people raise their children by not raising them is our problem. Guns killing people is our problem. You would not make the statement if the gun was pointing at you. Someone dying of hunger every three seconds is our problem. We may be fabulous, but until we collectively wake up, we are a planet that is depleting itself.

"It doesn't matter; I'm okay either way." This statement is made often, and I heard it a lot growing up in the South. When you asked people if they would like to have a chicken sandwich or a veggie burger, "It doesn't matter" is often the response you would hear. This becomes a pattern in people's lives, and it lacks the sense of empowerment that people deserve. What most people do not realize is that it becomes a habit, yet they say it so unconsciously and avoid making so many decisions.

What makes choosing so difficult in our society today is that we have more choices than ever. There are no longer just three movies playing at the theater or four pairs of shoes to choose from in a store. We are bombarded with so many choices that it's overwhelming. When people repeatedly say that it doesn't matter, their lives become an energy of indecisiveness, and indecisiveness is exhausting. It will take the energy from your body, and most important, indecisiveness is actually a decision, so when a person has the pattern of saying it doesn't matter, they are actually saying that *they* don't matter.

This is what they're saying: My uniqueness is not important, my originality is not significant, and therefore I'm barely just a something. I'm just a something that doesn't matter rather than being a unique contributor to society, to my family, and to the community.

We do have choices, and we make them according to the passions of our hearts. It's an entirely different story to be willing from time to time to compromise or to let somebody else choose, saying to your friend or family member, "You choose this time." Learn how to let go of saying it doesn't matter, because you matter, and this is the reason you were born. Miracle number one: you were born. Miracle number two: you allowed your true birth to occur.

"I will put on weight if I give up smoking and drinking." Our bodies do not punish us for returning to what is natural. The idea that they do is a tremendous shadow. We punish ourselves when we indulge in habits that our bodies are not designed to do long-term. It is our inner self-talk that gives us the results we really do not desire. A physical body with a vibrant breath going in and out of our lungs is not going to punish us; it will free us. For many years I have coached people who want to lose weight, and I have said to them, "Tell me how you talk to your body in front of the mirror several times a day. If you talked to your employee the way you talk to your body, your employee would quit. And this is what happens—your body quits on you."

We have often lied so much to our bodies that we are a promise undelivered. Our bodies no longer believe us and therefore do not respond. Think about it this way: if you make a promise to a child and you do not deliver, you will never hear the end of it.

Our bodies are shouting at times with red-energy ailments ready to be heard—a big old sigh for every lie, you might say. We make promises way too often to ourselves, our bodies, and our hearts, and we do not understand why life is not delivering the promises of heaven on Earth. We are working with the constant law "I get what I bring." When you bring truth and promises delivered, life will bring you the same.

"Money is not important. I don't really care about money, and I don't understand why people care so much about it." Money is an energy, and it is part of the way that we communicate in our society. People will say that money is the root of all evil, but have they ever stopped to really think that statement through? The actual biblical verse (1 Timothy 6:10) is that the *love* of money is the root of all evil. This doesn't necessarily mean that money will bring evil into our lives. Again, where is our responsibility? Perhaps that statement means it's the lack of understanding about money that causes people to live in a state of uncertainty. Evil doesn't always imply horror stories or concepts that are so big that movies can be made about them. Evil can simply be going against the grain of our lives.

If you look at the word *evil*, as I often tell people, it's *live* spelled backward (just as *devil* is *lived* spelled backward). I have found from my own experience that when people say money doesn't matter and they don't care about it, what they are really saying is that they have yet to understand how to create it for themselves and so therefore they are just disowning the reality that it can actually matter. There is so much judgment in our world about people who have money, yet if you desire to have an effect on the world at all—whether by saving animals, working to end pollution in our oceans, contributing to our planet in any way, or just being there for a neighbor—it takes money to do that.

Money is not the only thing that is important and significant, yet it matters a great deal. If we really believed it is our Creator's pleasure to give us the kingdom in the twenty-first century, we would celebrate having a way of communicating energy and abundance. We would celebrate being self-supportive and having the ability to offer solutions to causes in our lives. The issue is never money itself, but the limited belief that people have about money. I ask the universe to provide me with more money all the time, not because I need another thing but because it will give me the ability to use it to help empower someone, to feed a child, or to save an animal. I always tell people, "If you don't want more money, give it to me—I have lots of ways to use it." The truth sets us free when we are coming from the vibration of what is really true. As the author M. Scott Peck once said, "The truth is that our finest moments are most likely to occur when we are feeling deeply uncomfortable, unhappy, or unfulfilled. For it is only in such moments, propelled by our discomfort, that we are likely to step out of our ruts and start searching for different ways or truer answers."

Shadow Solutions

A number of years ago I traveled around the country for Pryor Resources and taught many classes offering tools for stress management. Pryor Resources collaborated with Richard Carlson, who authored the amazing books, *Don't Sweat the Small Stuff . . . and It's All Small Stuff*, *Don't Sweat the Small Stuff with Your Family*, and *Don't Sweat the Small Stuff at Work*.

Don't Sweat the Small Stuff . . . and It's All Small Stuff was one of the bestselling books of all time. I loved his material, and, since it is said that we teach what we are ready to hear, it was perfect for me to hear all this at that particular time in my life. I learned how to not sweat the small stuff and to realize that it was mostly all small stuff.

I started to develop my own tools to use when I would find myself getting dramatic about an event or a circumstance that most of the time I had little or no control over. I began to ask myself, *Is this going to be part of my forty-five-minute speech?* Is this issue, problem, or challenge really going to be mentioned in my eulogy? I created this after years of doing memorials and observing what is actually spoken within a forty-five-minute speech.

I would invite you to really explore and ponder this in a new way that is very true. Even if you are famous worldwide, you're only going to make two or three columns of the newspaper when you die. When you're famous, you will also get your photo published, but not necessarily the one you have chosen; you may be featured a few times on the news, but there are many things about this that are important to understand:

1. Unless you've written the article or speech, you have no control over what people are going to say.
2. You are at the mercy of how others have seen you, and this might not be how you saw yourself.
3. Rarely does anyone elaborate on where you worked, which really puts it into perspective, since we have made work such a big priority in our lives.
4. In twenty-five years of doing memorial services, I have never heard anyone talk about all the drama in a person's life.

Because of this and many other things, I realized that, when I am extremely stressed about a situation, it is important to ask myself, *Is this going to be part of my forty-five-minute memorial speech? How important is it, really, and is this worth my energy? Is it worth my health or my well-being? Is it worth my making myself sick?* It's not necessary for us to build condominiums of drama while we are walking through our shadows. The problem does not require our constant attention and stress. What should capture our attention is what we learn by discovering the solution that has always been there. Never does a problem exist without the solution already being there, and finding it is our quest. Our process is to discover how the solution can reveal itself in our lives.

If you have felt disconnected and drained, you are probably spending too much time as a worrier and a fixer and not enough time as a solver and a person who is empowering those around you. There is a huge difference between being a *caregiver* and being a *caretaker*. A caretaker takes issues on, whereas a caregiver gives others more life force by modeling vibrancy, praying, and holding sacred space. When you are a caretaker, you take away someone's right to be independent and make the person codependent with you.

What will make your forty-five-minute memorial speech? What do you want in your eulogy? Were you a lifter or a leaner? Were you acting as a lighthouse or always jumping in someone's rocky boat? Were you a builder of greatness or someone who was tearing down from weakness? This is one time in your life, though you have danced past your life, that it will matter.

A memorial service is where we teach future generations and ourselves the true value of how to live without dying and the deep need to feel rather than fill our shadows.

Our Deepest Shadow

One of our deepest shadows is our relationship to physical death. We deny death and run from it, as if by our doing so it will go away.

Plato said, "Who is more foolish, the child afraid of the dark or the adult afraid of the light?"

Every person who has had a near-death experience talks about going into the light. Then why are we so afraid to accept that we will owe life a death? Why are we so afraid of one day going into the light? Given our fascination with light shows and fireworks, you'd think that going into the light would sound like an incredible experience.

I have been on panels at assisted living facilities where I have spoken to the elderly about the value of owning their death, which is inevitable, and being a participant while they are cognizant in choosing what they would like at the end of their lives as their life celebration. They look at me as if I am out of my mind. Actually, in these moments I *am* out of my mind—I am in my heart. My heart has grieved for so many people I have loved throughout the years, and I've seen what their families choose for them when they are unable to choose for themselves. You would be appalled.

Here are some things to keep in mind:

- You will die, as will I.

- Unless you have in writing what will happen to your estate when you die, it will be decided for you. You have spent your whole life creating, and leaving all your creations behind will become chaotic unless you write your plans down. We fill out more paperwork to buy a house or adopt a pet than we do to honor an entire lifetime on this planet.

- If you really love the people you are leaving behind, please spare them the chaos of trying to figure out where all your papers are and putting together a plan when they have very little information to go on. Spend the little money it takes to plan now rather than the thousands it will take to keep the government from taking what you have spent your life accumulating.

- Do not give your children credit they have not earned by hoping they will work out your estate by themselves. The greedy children will want more, and the children who need what you had will never see it because the attorneys and time will waste it all away. What you avoid in your lifetime will unfairly be inherited by your children. Even if you know you can trust your children to be capable and competent, you should be aware that where death is concerned, even normally grounded people often become emotionally unstable.

- If you are religious or belong to a spiritual community and want to be honored a certain way, please write down all the details of your life celebration and give it to your attorney. Do not believe that people will grant you what you would have liked. They rarely do. I have seen so many families make decisions that have very little to do with the person who has died. It is not just because the family members are cold or do not care; they could just be emotionally distraught or totally unaware of the value you have placed on your spiritual preferences.

- Please have in writing that the minister, rabbi, or leader is not to use your death to promote his or her own philosophy and religious values to get new people to come to that place of worship. Your life celebration is to be about *you*. Please spread the word that any talk not about you is absolutely unacceptable.

I will always remember going to a funeral of a friend's mother. My friend had been a member of my community for many years, and her mom had belonged to the Baptist church in the city. I was so energized when I walked into the funeral home and discovered that the woman's favorite colors were displayed: red, black, and gold. She had requested something special at her service and for her ride to her next life: a red casket. It was incredible to see this. It made me think of my red Mercedes and how much I love that car.

It shifted the paradigm of yet another person in the same type of brown box. Really, you would think that we would get a little fancier about the event that marks our departure from Earth. Seeing how this woman planned her exit was so uplifting and meaningful—until the minister took advantage of her favorite colors by using them to promote his Baptist philosophy. He preached away that red was Jesus's blood, black was the devil, and gold was for the few who would get to see heaven. Then he proceeded to talk about a book his church had made that explained all these ideas, and by the way, don't forget to visit us. We are located at . . .

I was appalled! Are you kidding me? Who was going to talk

about the woman? This was her event, her life, and her years of contributing to society. This was not supposed to be a marketing plan to develop a church. Please, we must change.

Your end-of-life celebration should be as exciting as the day you were born. Go out with a bang! The more you accept your death, the more valuable your day-to-day life will be.

Recently I heard about New Orleans socialite Mickey Easterling and her desires when she was writing her last will and testament. Before she passed away at age eighty-three, she made sure that she would attend the last party she ever planned—her own wake. Rather than being put in a typical brown box or an urn for all to pass by and see, she stipulated that she was to be sitting up, as if she were at one of her many parties. Her eyes were closed, and she had a drink in her hand. Although her soul had left her body, this was a positive way for people to visit her and pay their respects. It gave them the feeling of living rather than the typical dread and pain of dying.

We can move from relation to translation to transformation, if we are willing to understand the valleys and mountains of day-to-day life and how crucial it is to understand that death is a shadow. Through our ability to seek the light, the shadow will always be behind us rather than in front of us. When we can have healthy conversations about dying within, the death on the outside will not feel like the final curtain call.

So let's look at the shadow we have concerning death and how we handle the dead. On my radio show I once interviewed a funeral director who was very well-known in his field, and we had an incredible discussion about how we treat those who have died. We both asked, "What is the rush to bury the dead for the funeral or for a memorial after cremation?" Actually, there is no reason why a person who dies on Sunday has to be buried by Wednesday. We still are driven by an era in which we had to bury the dead quickly because their bodies would begin to smell.

Here we are in the twenty-first century, rushing this process without properly going through the emotions and allowing people time to decide what is best. Usually we are so focused on all the details that we do not have time to sit and feel anything. We rush as if we were in a race to get it done, to get all the details and the planning complete. It usually takes people a lot longer to accept what has occurred because of the lack of ritual, which would have helped with the death of a loved one (whether an animal or a person).

Please take the time to plan out your service. When my father died unexpectedly, we were very rushed to have him buried within a couple of days and to put the experience "behind" us. I was very heartsick, for the loss was deeper than I ever imagined. My heart felt as if it were cracking open. It hurt physically, a true heartache. For the first time, I truly understood sad songs about a broken heart. I got it—when you are experiencing it, it is truly real and painful.

Losing my dad happened during one of the few times I was employed at a corporation. I was a recruiter and was making the company a lot of money. You would have thought I had taken the summer off when I took just a few business days to support my family, take care of my father's business, and put myself together as best I could to face the public again. The people I worked for were so heartless and cold; they constantly reminded me about how many days I had been out of work. They did not care about me; they only cared about their money. Their true colors shined through, and I left that job immediately. In my opinion, if you do not honor death, then you will never honor life.

The other shocking experience I witnessed involved a woman who had passed away in another southern state, and the family had called her church for the priest do a service. This woman and her husband were a well-known couple who had greatly contributed to the medical field and to the opera and theater. It took the priest almost three days to let the family know that he declined to hold the service because the deceased had not contributed to the parish in recent years. I could not believe it. How could an organization called Holy Name of Jesus be so lacking in standards? I thought this church needed to spend some time looking at its branding, for the holy name of Jesus or another adored deity would have done better by this family.

When a church was finally found for the service, the priest sprinkled holy water on the woman in the casket and made a declaration granting her permission to go to heaven. Really? Who has the power to grant another human being admission to heaven? Have we succumbed to playing God?

Just as the priest stated his decree, there was thunder, and it was so loud it almost moved the sanctuary. It was amazing! I kid you not. It was as if the woman were saying to the priest, "First of all, you don't have this right, and second, I am already there!"

Please know that you are not robotic in nature, and you do not have to settle for these types of end-of-life celebrations. You can make requests and be clear about what you are going to do for yourself and your loved ones.

The more we value our deaths, the more we accept our lives as unique by design.

I say the following at every memorial or funeral: Death is our most avoided reality, and until we embrace it, we will never have the capacity to truly live. Think about the people who are not afraid to die. Think about the people who welcome death with bravery—the people who truly live and do not avoid death.

I was recently with the film crew that is creating a promotional video for this book. One of the sets was in a cemetery, and we were all mindful of not "walking on the dead." I thought how interesting it is that many of us are more concerned with not walking on the dead than we are with waking up the walking dead to be truly alive. There are a lot of people on Earth today who are walking and going through the motions, yet energetically they are dead. The good news is they can become awakened and be alive again.

If you are the parent, grandparent, relative, friend, teacher, practitioner, or preacher of anyone who appears to be dying while living, you may wonder what you can do to help the person. The most important thing you can do is to become more alive yourself and bring more light into your life. Light will illuminate the shadows and darkness and create a sense of permanent change more easily than words will. You are doing the person an immense disservice when you adjust your vibrant energy to make him or her feel comfortable, and you are also sabotaging your own awakening, for the more you lower your standards, the more apt you are to meet those low standards.

The Biggest Shadow of All

Is there a devil? Do you really believe there is a bogeyman out to get you?

We've already discussed that *devil* is *lived* spelled backward. The devil, in our society, is considered to be an external force that makes us do bad things. Talk about a scapegoat—the poor guy is always being blamed for what *we* choose to do. "The devil made me do it," people say. Really? Are we so pathetic that we cannot own the fact that we simply make choices and that some of our choices are better than others?

When are we ever going to grow up? When I blame, I cannot claim my life, my energy, my possibilities, or my well-being. Let's give this devil guy a rest—we are simply living backward.

Even if there were a false shadow guy who causes us to sin, do you know what *sin* really means? It means to miss the mark, as in archery. We do from time to time miss the mark in our lives by living backward, living in the past, not correcting a mistake, and we fall short of our infinite possibilities. Choices that we make by allowing animal cruelty and adding to current pollution challenges are just a couple of examples of how we as humans miss the mark and could truly do better.

We know better, but we are not doing better. Our world is at a crucial point, and we need all major faiths to unite their believers at a new level of spiritual action, a place beyond knowing. We need to stop spending our time belittling people into believing that they cannot have a relationship with God and instead teach them how to have a relationship with what God is creating, including themselves. We continue to destroy our planet by destroying creation, and therefore we are destroying one another.

We have been missing the mark, and we are way past the point at which Noah and one boat can save us. We are experiencing cause and effect of wasting life, either with the creatures on our planet or as the walking dead. Until we redeem ourselves by waking up to honoring life, our lives will not be honored, and we will continue to murder our own. We are uncreating creation.

"Truly, I say to you, as you did not do it to one of the least of these, you did not do it to me" (Matthew 25:45).

As we stop killing what we do not eat, as we stop being fascinated with something that will make a good news story and instead evolve to our own story, we will come closer to being awake and actually feeling good. We need our knowing to match our growing and our showing.

Here's the truth: The devil did not make us do it; we did it to ourselves. Let's mature, for God's sake (pun intended).

Can sin, which implies missing the mark, be much more simplified? There are big unkind acts and small unkind acts, but maybe not all unkind acts have a rippling effect. For example, is it an unkind act to forget to bring cloth bags to the grocer and depend on plastic bags when we know the deleterious effects of using so much plastic? We all need to have "plastic surgery"—that is, we need to have all the plastic removed from our houses and our stores and start to wake up. We have a plastic problem, which is interesting because a lot of people have become plastic themselves, in the sense of not real and inauthentic. When we know better yet do not do better, this is definitely a wrong we are doing to ourselves.

The definition of a shadow is also very simple. A shadow is all the "almost moments"—events that could have been but that we missed while we were sleeping. We missed the mark. We missed the moment. The devil didn't do it; we did it to ourselves, and often we do it to one another.

When we accept that something is only a shadow, not only do we free ourselves from everyday bondage, loss of energy, and despair, we also move ahead to take our sacred stories into the future. It is important to know who we truly are as divine creations, including all the aspects of ourselves that we may label good or bad, beautiful or ugly. We cannot long for a world of coexistence, oneness, and improved distribution if we are continuously separated from ourselves by denying our shadows and our humanity.

We cannot represent the integrity of our being if we say we believe in a world of oneness but do not accept the oneness in our humanity and make peace with the oneness within ourselves. Once we awaken and become true to who we are again, we will see a brighter world. Geniuses and nerds will totally wipe out world hunger before being concerned with one more game or toy; we will not murder our own, because the inner punishment will exceed any prison cell; doctors will again care about their patients and ask questions rather than telling patients their futures like minigods; teachers will actually teach by modeling what they are saying; ministers and priests will be sober and have their addictions transformed into true self-care rather than displaying them weekly in front of people who are robotic; a church will actually be one for all people from all faiths and all walks of life; only parents who are not children will have children; we will evolve from being childish to being childlike again; bankers will have an interest in you as a person instead of caring about the financial interest they can take from you. Our government will offer solutions from a new paradigm, and we will see an entire transformation of our planet.

We are living in an amazing time. We need more people to honor our creation stories by being creative thinkers. We have the potential to truly discover our abilities to do miracles. When we realize the secret to making a shadow disappear is simply to understand and embody the way we stand in the light, we will be free. We will live in the truth, and our energy will be laser-focused rather unevenly dispersed.

How can we get better? First we admit that we need to wake up, and then we wake up. We begin to live in a more practical way. We are willing to go in a new direction, for the choices we have made have only brought us this far. When you wish upon a star, it does make a difference who you are. When we begin to live in truth and stop accepting insane realities—such as that we are forever doomed because someone was not supposed to eat an apple at creation—we will rise to the greatest light humanity has ever known.

Stop trying to teach the pig to sing—it will make you angry, and it annoys the pig.

Ideas to Process and Integrate

~~≈≈◦◯◦≈≈~~

Most people are dying a little every day because they are attempting to use an old map that doesn't have the new road on it. Many people stopped using their "thinker and soul voice" and adapted to what someone else felt or said, which may be true for one person yet not true for another.

Are any of your daily habits or rituals keeping you from going down a new road? If so, what are they? On what shadows in your life have you built condominiums? Where have you built walls rather than bridges? When you read the list of clichés we say to ourselves, which ones do you use, and how can you feel more empowered by changing the way you respond to specific challenges in your life? How do you frame events so they do not cause extreme stress?

What do you want spoken at your eulogy? Is this how you are living and being now?

What situation can you be free from right now? Take the time to write it down, and observe the changes in your body. Allow this process to become a ritual for responding to small and large moments in your life.

The more we value our deaths, the greater we accept our lives as unique by design.

When you wish upon a star, it does make a difference who you are.

Allow yourself to be in front of your shadows.

8

Moving Beyond Energy

Step Eight: How to Live Awake, Full, and Present

Are you awake yet? Are you waking up? Have you learned how to stop dying every day? Are you moving from fear to freedom, providing a new download to your GPS and restoring all parts of your soul? Are you celebrating your birthday as the real you? Are you going places with the new you? Are you learning that your dreams are waiting on you to come true and transcending your shadows? Are you ready now to move beyond energy and to live fully awake and present?

There is one more thing I believe you must know: You must change more than your thinking. You must open your heart.

Maya Angelou said, "I've learned that whenever I decide something from an open heart, I usually make the right decision."

So how do you begin now to live? You open your heart by changing your energy so your life will change. The flow of life cannot reach you if you are blocked with layers and layers of protection, the attitudes of a fixed position, and the unwillingness to start waking up and be willing to change.

You are the one you have been waiting for. This must be clear within every part of you. If you want something different, then you must be different and not continue to have the same people validate you so you stay the same.

You will never move forward by repeating what is in back of you. The people in your huddle are comfortable with you staying the same. When you change, the whole game plan can change.

My mom knows that her health would benefit if she lost ten to fifteen pounds, yet her knowing that has not moved her to growing and showing it. She said to me one day, "My friends are saying to me that I am thin enough and I shouldn't lose any weight." I said to her, "Mom, of course they will say that to you. To them you are thin because they weigh over two hundred pounds." And then I reminded her of all the alcoholics who told me in my late twenties that I did not have a drinking problem.

The small percentage of people who are awake and who practice "change your thinking, change your life" appear to be further along than the people who are not changing anything or the people who are walking along and feeling like nothing is happening at all.

I started looking around me in my thirties and listening to the stories of people who told me they were changing their thinking, but I realized that their lives weren't changing that much. They meant well, yet they were not changing well. I could see that at first individual lights would go on and they would have major shifts, but then very little happened after the first surge of growth. They may have attracted new jobs with more pay, yet they still had financial challenges. They may have attracted better lovers than they had before, and they may even have looked better, yet they still were not happy. We have become a society of many people immersed in self-help with the mantra of "change your thinking, change your life," yet have our lives really changed much? And if our lives actually have changed much and we are such a self-helping culture, then why does it appear that we have not really helped ourselves?

We have sold a lot of products and bought a lot of books, but doesn't it seem to you that it's the same crowd over the past few years that has gone to the same programs, participated in the same book clubs, and watched the same self-improvement videos?

So what is missing? Too much education and not enough integration could be one reason we have not helped ourselves in this self-help world. We haven't gone deep enough to truly integrate what we have intellectually learned.

What I am expressing has changed my life and can change your life. I have learned to embody the truth from the energy of an open heart. A trained mind creates an open heart. Changing our thinking is absolutely necessary, but it is just the beginning of deep spiritual maturity. We must go deeper into our hearts. In order to get to the heart of the matter, we must go to the heart to discover what matters.

Let me repeat: We are not here to play God; we are here to show ourselves and others how to allow God to play through us by expressing our original selves and demonstrate miracles.

The physical heart is connected to the emotional body. People die of heartache. People die of a broken heart. Heart issues are listed in Peter Russell's World Clock as the number one reason for death in our society. It is heart issues that take most lives in our culture. And it is the reason so many people are living as the walking dead—their hearts are not feeling and revealing.

Therefore, a real quest for people committed to self-improvement is to help the self by healing the wounds of the emotional body. These are the wounds that we carry and project over and over in our lives until we heal and reveal them. When more and more individuals really heal their emotional bodies and open their hearts, they will step into their true authentic power and be change agents for our society. They will move from trying to perfect the same ideas over and over again to deepening the inner connection with themselves and others. They will be able to soar rather than sabotage. They will discover they are eagles rather than chickens.

Here's another idea to be aware of: the self-help industry is ready for people who have helped themselves to accept from an open heart that they are enough and who can claim their right and value to bring the changes we need to our world. The archetypes of the heart regarding the fourfold way, offered by Angeles Arrien, are some of the best material I have ever read, studied, and embodied. You will learn in this material that the shadow of the healer archetype is perfection. A healer's shadow is that I need to be perfect first. There are a lot of people who are capable of moving forward and being change agents who go to one more seminar or get one more degree or credential because their shadow won't accept that they "got it." Their shadow of perfection prevents the heart of connection.

We therefore have two situations that we can shift. The people who are knowing (in the mind) yet are not moving into growing and showing (in the emotional body and the heart) can go deeper and discover their true messages, to change their world first and then change ours.

The people who have made the shift but who still entertain the shadows of perfection and control can transform, enlighten, and totally affect humanity through deeper shadow work with the heart archetypes.

You start where you are. We all can benefit our society by starting today. This day will affect our tomorrow.

Leading from the Heart

When we learn to lead from the heart rather than the head, we will have true leaders who can bring humanity into a deeper awareness of spirituality.

Maybe public speaking isn't your gift. Maybe counseling or being a life coach isn't your gift, either. Maybe it's organization or a green thumb or the desire to be the logistics coordinator, giving people rides to your local event. Each could be your arena of leadership. And remember the one butterfly who flaps his wings across the globe is felt by us. We are all affected by the actions of everyone else.

Sometimes it seems we have too many people who truly need to help themselves before they can fully help others. Some people attempt to help others too soon on their own healing journeys. We all may know a few of these folks, who get a business card and a website and make great claims before they have completed their own life training program.

Anyone who wants to be a teacher should ask him- or herself the following: Am I walking my talking? Am I modeling my message? If I am making claims about relationships, am I in a relationship? If I am sharing advice about money, do I have some money? If I claim to understand *The Secret* (which is not a secret) by Rhonda Byrne, do I manifest what the book and the movie say? And will any secret be permanent if I do not allow God's creation of me to become actualized? Will my life magnify my Creator if the discovery of my own potential remains a secret to myself?

All of us can help our society by holding ourselves to high standards. This does not mean holding someone accountable for what he or she said twenty-five years ago. This is unnatural and spiritually wrong. Who among us doesn't have issues we have needed to forgive and asked to be forgiven from twenty-five years ago? These types of issues cause an insanity that saps our energy because they bring up the feeling (from a deep layer of the emotional body) that we do not deserve to be forgiven. It costs all of us the ability to believe that life moves forward rather than backward. And when we as a society are part of the process by publicly seeing people put down because of something they said more than twenty-five years ago, we are all zapped at our core because it feeds our own feeling that we are unforgivable and cannot move forward.

That we are such an unforgiving society prevents many would-be great leaders from stepping up. We pick people to run our world whom we want to have a flawless past, so they can help humanity with its issues. Does this make sense? Wouldn't you want a global leader who has walked through shadows, pain, challenges of life, and other problems and has proved how to do it so that he or she will not be separate from the rest of humanity? Are we naive enough to believe that a person whom we create to be separate from us by having a flawless résumé is going to have empathy and solutions to problems that he or she is separate from?

Résumés do not make leaders—life does. True leaders move us forward, not backward.

We have problems like obesity (the slow death of the self), profanity (the slow death of energy), murdering our own (the slow and immediate death of humanity), and addiction, which takes away our present and our presents, or spiritual gifts (slow suicide), yet we are often fixated on something someone said one-quarter of a century ago.

Please, dear God, let us have our knowing becoming our growing and finally our showing.

We cannot take shortcuts on our eternal journey; when we do, people who are in our circle of influence feel shortchanged. It's time to start waking up and living every day. It's time to wake up and *be life*!

Energetic Words of Life

The world is aching for people to speak intelligently about life's issues. It doesn't matter if you believe there are no economic issues; many people believe there are. Rather than make them feel ignorant, show them how you are not affected rather than telling them the issues do not exist. Show them not with chatty words but with real evidence in your life. I do not believe in growing old, but many people start talking at forty about how old they feel. They believe, along with many others, that growing old is a fact of life. It is their fact of life because they believe it. My way of teaching truth is to show them an ageless spirit, not correct their words, which just annoys the pig and makes them angry. Words can at times shift people's consciousness, yet setting an example works much better. Setting an example has lasting results. They can see it; therefore, they can believe it.

You can tell people there is no duality, but they will look at you very confused. You can say there isn't good and evil, but to affect society we must prove that there is only one Presence and Power in the universe and that anything else is our misuse of this understanding. We will change our world by proving there is no separation, not by separating ourselves—by walking our talking, not just by talking.

Another area where we as a society have totally changed and decreased our energy is our everyday language. When I was growing up, only two or three people around me used profanity, and it always turned me off. I could read energy back then, and I could see that when people cursed, their energy lessened in their bodies.

My father used to curse my younger brother, and as a result my brother has spent many years of his life proving to himself that he is not a curse. I could see the aura of my father become gray and the light around his heart begin to weaken. His light actually dimmed. And then he'd eat more sugar.

Short-term, profanity may seem cute and funny to some and give them a false feeling of power, but long-term, it depletes the energy of your body. Some people say they hope we do not lose the English language, but I say that in some ways we already have. We go to movies that are so filled with profanity that you cannot even tie the key ideas together. We are being sold negativity of the lowest vibration and dehumanization, and we are buying it. We are lowering our standards and therefore our energy. This combination of cursing and denying the self is putting us under a curse of dying every day and not fully living.

If you are an influencer to anyone, please use the F-word *freedom* and lose the other F-word in your day-to-day language, along with all other words that lower your vibration. It is not a religious issue, it is a spiritual issue. It keeps people from truly being self-actualized, for it keeps bringing a lower vibration and pulling them backward rather than moving them forward. Our society needs help to truly get back to the land of the living, so please offer your energy by expressing yourself from a higher vibration and using words that are uplifting rather than insecure and demeaning.

Energetic Food and Water

For many years, people have asked me to share my views on how to go beyond seeing and viewing life to actually *being* life: being present, intentional, and alive. People are always asking me, "How do you have so much energy?" I realized early on in my talks—whether they were about spirituality, sexuality, sobriety, or stress management—that there was always a strong element related to energy.

I have shared tools for being fully alive with many great minds, authors, and teachers on my radio show "The Intentional Spirit."

How much energy do we have? What people or things drain our energy, and what people or things give us energy?

Years ago I considered the message I believed I was here to impart; I was certain that if I was going to talk about energy, then I really needed to have some. With that awareness, I made a decision that once I was on the other side of every event that occurred in my life, I would be more energetic than I had been before. I was clear that I would have more energy than I knew what to do with. I would be like the Energizer Bunny, a truly impassioned and energized being.

I set out to move my life from being disconnected and drained to being impassioned and energized. Once I considered the decision to do so, change became necessary, and the decision to "do and be" allowed more energy to follow.

I came to believe that the energy we die with ought to be the same amount of energy we were born with—and even more, actually. I came to believe that it wasn't growing older that was taking my energy, it was that I had never truly been me that was taking my energy. I was giving the world only small doses of me, a little at a time, and therefore I was getting only small doses of the life force in return. I wasn't truly living, so life wasn't truly giving in return.

This was a true High-way adjustment for me, since I came from a small town with a small awareness of nutrition and self-care. My day started with toast, butter, and sugar and continued with sugar snacks throughout the day. School lunch contained lots of carbs and more sugar, and when I arrived at home there was soda and sweetened tea (which meant a little tea in my sugar) and lots of fried foods.

I recall one day when all I had were several glasses of milk followed by large chunks of cheese. Nutritious, right? Fresh vegetables were sometimes available, yet usually our vegetables were in cans in the cabinet. Canned beans and veggies were dressed up with oily spices and perhaps a ham bone that once belonged to a precious pig. This is what we called "eating right" back then.

We put more of an effort into setting the table than we did in what we were putting into our mouths. Soon in my youth we were introduced to fast food, or, as I now call it, past food. It's not what I consider food anymore.

This eating pattern continued throughout my childhood, until I moved away from home and expanded into a much larger world.

All the wonderful exposure to sugar toast, sugar sweets, and sugar sodas led to the need to be filled by alcohol. I used to tell people that I did not eat sweets, and I really didn't, but I would have half a bottle of wine instead, and this went on for a number of years. When I became sober at twenty-nine, I then craved sugar and sweets all the time, trying to get the same fix.

This I've learned: We are a society addicted to sugar, then we crave alcohol, and now we have added special sugar coffee drinks. Since coffee for some people carries the energy of anger, when you add sugar (more anger), what do you get?

Road rage, violence, big people snapping at little people, people screaming at each other—probably 35 to 45 percent of our dysfunction would be eliminated if we were wise enough to change what we put into our physical bodies.

I am not willing to coach or work as a shaman with people who are not willing to change the way they eat and drink. It is a waste of their time and mine.

A long-term sugarholic is equivalent to a rage-aholic, with lots of red-anger energy in the body. Often long-term red energy in the body creates or feeds fibromyalgia, cancer, and inflammatory diseases like arthritis and diverticulitis. Please note, however, that I am an intuitive healer and not a medical practitioner, and I am not saying that one size fits all. I am also not saying that sugar is the only cause, but it certainly does not help the condition.

The challenge is allowing the change. It's like a very dirty sponge: when you clean it, you pour water over and over it, squeezing it, draining it, and washing it some more—you cannot believe how much dirt is in the sponge. Because so many people have eaten processed food, sugar, and dairy for so long, their sponge is very dirty, and you cannot know how dirty it is until you cease to do it for a certain amount of time. It is only after you get sugar, for example, out of your system that you can truly understand what it is doing to you physically and emotionally.

I can still have sugar on a rare occasion; it feels great going in, but afterward I usually regret it. I usually don't sleep well that night, and the next day I have more extreme emotions. It truly changes me, as it changes many people—they just aren't tuned into it.

My friend Caroline Sutherland is brilliant in teaching about our bodies and how sugar feeds cancer. I am so grateful for the effect she has had on my health, my well-being, and most of all, my energy. The more I committed to no longer being drained and feeling disconnected, the more I needed to change my eating program. I stopped regularly drinking soda in my thirties, I rarely had it in my forties, and I have had none at all in the past few years. I didn't just wake up one day and decide never to do this or that again, but when I stopped drinking soda I knew it was permanent, good-bye forever, and when I stopped smoking I knew that until I saw a squirrel and a bird smoke a cigarette, I was not going to, either.

I started drinking room-temperature Pi Water, which is living mineralized water, and that's been my liquid program ever since. You drink the number of ounces that is half the numerical value of your body weight; so, for example, if you weigh 150 pounds, you would drink 75 ounces, or about nine cups, of water every day. (This is in addition to the water content in coffee, tea, or soup.) The first thing I do after my prayers and rituals in the morning is to drink a full glass of room-temperature water. I was tested a couple of years ago by a practitioner, and she said I was the most hydrated person she has ever tested. I told her it was because I had been using a special water filtering system for more than fifteen years. I also use a special shower head, and when I travel I usually take these things with me.

Here I am, a person who almost killed myself by the way I fed my body with junk, now a dedicated health advocate. Wow—in one lifetime. That's a miracle right there.

In addition to drinking half your numeric body weight every day in fluid ounces of water, eat half your numeric body weight every day in grams of protein. When you crave sugar, your body needs more protein. Thank you, Caroline Sutherland!

The more I worked on my emotional body and my energy increased, the more I could no longer eat certain foods. It would always become very evident, for I would get sick, either nauseous or with flulike systems. The body would rid itself of the toxins, and then I would not be able to go back to what I had previously been eating. If you are not in touch with your body, you will tend to blame the effects of certain foods on outside factors, but once you are in a rhythm, it becomes very easy to discern the true cause. After you give your body a break from your cravings, then over time, even if you do go back and have a sugar delight or big old bag of carbs, you will wish it out of your body, for it no longer feels natural. I am usually a few carbs away from way too many, and what I have observed over the years is that carbs decrease my energy level. I still eat them at times, but the key is awareness. I am aware of what I eat and whether it gives me energy or depletes my energy.

Some nutritionists say that wheat and dairy are two of the most overpromoted and least healthy items we can put into our bodies. I do not see any nutritional value in these two food categories. Often it is not the product itself, but what is put into it to lengthen its shelf life that causes the problem. I look back now at all my allergic reactions, all the testing my parents put me through when I was a child, and all the times I was told I had hay fever and other things. All of it went away when I stopped eating dairy and processed foods. I think of processed foods like packaged meats in the fridge or types of food in cans in addition to foods in a box. When you are shopping, always look at the ingredients on the back. The more ingredients there are, the less value the food will have for you.

Here's what I recommend: Always be willing to take something out of your diet for thirty days and then add it back in. Our bodies are like sponges; if you don't totally clean them, you won't realize the gunk that is in there. Once you take a break from something and then add it back, you will get the full experience of what it does to you.

A request from your body for a shift in diet happens to people all the time, yet because they are not in tune with their bodies, they write it off as something that is unnecessary or just a new fad. But it's your body going through a new phase of lightening up, and the universe is sending you clues. The body itself is not robotic, as some of us are, so it will never lie. If you continue to lie to it, it will make you lie down.

I was surrounded by people who went completely by what the doctor said. When I was six and started sneezing, my tribe said to me, "You probably will have asthma like your grandmother."

"What is that?" I said. I couldn't spell it, but it didn't sound too promising. When I was thirteen and having cramps as part of my blessed karma of being a girl, my tribe told me that I would probably have to have a hysterectomy like my aunt. What is that?

There is no telling where I would be—or whether I would "be" at all—if I had not had enough common sense and wisdom to listen inwardly and follow my own path about my body. And even though in the early years I was a total sugar addict, I still knew when something I was being told wasn't going to influence my decisions. I had several doctors throughout the years who wanted to do sinus surgery or female surgery on me, and I knew it wasn't right.

I would go back to the doctor who brought me into the world. He would always work me into his schedule, and I would sit with all the newborns in the lobby. I must have been close to twenty when he told me I really needed to move on. I had trusted him so much, and he spared me many senseless surgeries and body drama. He was one of the few people I had ever met who knew that the body had the potential to naturally heal itself of certain ailments and discomforts.

In the next chapter of my life, I was still eating fish and chicken, but over time I found I could do neither one. I have been almost vegan for many years, except that I still eat eggs. But by the time you read this, I might not be doing that anymore, either.

I drink three or four protein shakes a day from pea protein, not soy or whey. I also make a large fresh vegetable smoothie each day with fresh ginger root and turmeric. I use kale and lots of other greens, carrots, beets, cilantro, a small amount of ice, and protein.

I really notice a difference when I travel to places where I am not able to do juicing. My energy begins to shift a great deal until I can find some fresh vegetable juice.

I use protein powder from trusted suppliers (see the resource section at the back of the book). By making this simple change, I have exponentially increased my energy.

It is very crucial that you read the amount of carbohydrates and sugar on everything. There are a lot of good popular brands of food, but if you read the small print, you will see that they are loaded with sugar and carbs. A great exercise is to go thirty days with no (or hardly any) carbs, and then have some carbs some afternoon. They will be delicious going down, but you will be sleepy within a few minutes.

Healthy food costs more, but it will save you thousands of dollars and lots of anguish and pain in the long run. We are always going to spend money; it is part of the rent we pay to be a human being. It is better to spend it on the things that make us feel good and support us in valuing our lives.

Every couple of years I also do an extensive body cleansing that cleans out all my organs. I use gentle herbs, which work naturally with the body. I always feel so much younger and lighter when I invest the few weeks required to do the program. We need society to change in how it views health costs. My insurance will pay for me to take as many flu shots as I want, which I would never put into my body, yet it will not pay for the only thing I currently use: B_{12} injections. That seems wrong.

Over the years, I have invested lots of time, effort, and money to take care of my physical house. I also sleep with a mattress with magnets and have air systems throughout my home. I am committed to my energy staying forever young.

At times you will want to talk yourself into going the cheaper route, yet if you resist this, on a long-term basis you will feel amazing and will love being an impassioned and energetic human being. What you save short-term will not save you long-term.

I can clearly see that cancer became common in our society after two other things had become common: (1) microwave ovens, and (2) plastic containers instead of glass. Most of our liquids, such as juices, are in thin plastic, and most of it sits on a hot truck as it moves from state to state.

I use my built-in microwave oven to tell time, and that's all. If you ever overheat something in a microwave, you will clearly see what you are putting in your body. It kills the food and the nutrients.

We seem to believe that all bottled water comes from fresh springs, but most does not, and even when it does, it sits in plastic containers filled with chemicals until it reaches you. The simplest thing to do is to buy a large glass bottle and have your own filtering system. Fill the bottle twice a day. This way you will remember what you have had to drink, and you won't have to second-guess if you have had enough water.

People will often say this is hard, yet once you start, it will be harder *not* to do it. It will change your energy, and as you change your energy, your life will change. You will be a difference maker and attract more life to yourself. You will not need to know a special formula to attract what you want into your life, for you will be an attraction magnet.

Health Is Wealth

Health is wealth. Yet strong societal forces encourage trusted doctors to become drug pushers, especially to the patient who may not want to make the necessary lifestyle changes. But we should at least let the patient know that there is a choice between serious side effects and good health.

I have not taken even an aspirin for the past ten years or so. I am very sensitive to anything pharmaceutical. I had some work done on my teeth, and the dentist gave me a pain pill that would have put a horse down. I was out—in another place for two or three days. Please check the side effects of any medicines you are given by a doctor. We are bombarded with the advertising mantra to "check with your doctor first before taking this or any medication." What I am saying is to please check *after* your doctor, before you take anything.

A few years ago, a man was having difficulty with a runny nose, and the doctor wanted to do surgery on him. I asked him one day to tell me what medications he was taking, and all three medications had the side effect of a runny nose. I asked him whether he had been told about this, and he said no.

Putting time and energy into your own care and well-being is crucial if you want to thrive and be a vibrant person. You are worth the energy this takes.

As a spiritual leader, I encourage the health of all those around me. I've noticed too many operations on joints and too much back pain. Can this be avoided?

Our knees and feet are perfectly designed to hold the weight of our bodies and keep us grounded. Flip-flops, which your feet slide into, do not offer you the heel-to-toe push the body is designed to have, and many people are having knee problems as a result. I had this experience personally, for I had all these supposedly "sexy" shoes with high heels or no strap in the back, so I started to have a major challenge with my right knee. Once I started wearing the right shoes, the knee pain went away.

And if you are a few pounds overweight and are considering surgery for joint replacement, please lose the weight first. It would truly serve everyone to lose weight before doing anything major, and all surgery is major.

Children are especially under attack today. Most children are given sugar every day for the first few years of their lives, and many are given medication to calm them down. Sugar hypes you up—more people, I hope, will learn to make the connection. Children today are not the same as the baby boomers were as children; they are energetically different and cannot be given the same diet as in the 1950s, with its heavy dependence on sugar and white flour.

We also need to stop medicating genius children so they can adjust to public school. Instead we need to look at our worn-out model of education. The system was in desperate need of change when I was a student and bored. We can be confident that it still needs to change. Lori L. Desautels, the author of *How May I Serve You? Revelations in Education*, makes many good suggestions about our education system.

I was such a bright child, and my lack of nutrition was destroying me. I was scolded for being so hyper. If I were a child today, I'd be heavily medicated.

There are various support systems that I have used for many years, and I encourage you to check these out for yourself and your loved ones:

- MAT—muscle activation techniques by Liz Swayne for a balanced system.
- Orthogonal chiropractic, which changed my spine's alignment as well as the way my intentions are aligned.
- Homeopathy, one of the most ancient forms of remedies; good for both you and your pets.
- Acupuncture for individuals and for pets.
- Bach flower remedies and herbs, also for both you and your pets.
- Cumin, turmeric, lemon juice, ghee, and coconut oil in your food.
- Muscle testing, which is crucial until you learn to trust yourself.
- A doctor who is truly a friend and who will be honest rather than someone you worship.
- A live blood analysis, so you can see what areas of your life you can adjust to be totally healthy. (A live blood analysis is very different than a blood analysis.)

And here's a final health alert for all the animals we know and love: our dogs and cats are changing. They have been home dwellers for many generations now, and to feed them chemicals year after year is causing them great physical challenges. They are showing signs of rage, seizures, and various illnesses. We are causing them to die a little because of what we are putting into their bodies.

Four years ago, a woman called me and asked me to see her dog. She knew I was an intuitive healer and a shamanic practitioner, and I was her last resort. Her beautiful golden retriever was only two years old and had been a show dog. She was on medication because she was having seizures, and this amazing and lively animal spent her days sleeping in her bed. When Gemma first came into my office, I showed her a new dog toy, and her owner, Terri, said, "She doesn't play with toys; she never has."

Gemma lay on the floor in my office, and I lay down beside her. I told her, "This is the day your life is going to change!" I told her she was safe and that I could hear her. On an intuitive level, she told me that "they" do not know what they are doing. I listened to her, then I called my homeopathic vet, and he and Terri talked on the phone. I had told Terri that Gemma was probably getting too many vaccinations, and the homeopathic vet agreed that this was the case.

He shared with her what to do and told her he would mail her the remedies. I said to Gemma, "Honey, you can now get back to living." She took the toy I had offered her and joyfully carried it to the van with her mom. She also took with her a new life. Gemma is now a show dog again, touching lives as she was created and destined to do.

True wealth is health, for health is the only area in our lives that we cannot fake. All other benefits of being a human being do not exceed good health. I am very grateful to all the people who have taught me wisdom about my body and how to take care of it. I have had many influencers, and I thank you for my vibrant life. If I have failed to mention you and give you credit for my knowledge, know that it was not intentional. I did not fail to listen to you, and I am grateful.

Teachers and Healers

How did I get from A to B—*A* being eating Almost everything, and *B* being what is Best for my energy level? How did I go from the destroyer over the years to the focused eater and supplement taker? How did I go from fried and tired to organic and dynamic?

For more than twenty years I have lived by the motto to "pay attention to what knocks on my door three times." When I hear someone say something he or she is doing, and then this happens a couple more times, I know it is mine to do as well. My intuition feels the invitation, and I get a huge *yes*, this is mine to do.

When my shaman teacher, Berenice Andrews, appeared in my life, she taught me for years about the unified energy field. She also taught me about certain foods and how I needed to change not only what was eating me (mentally) but also what I was eating. I learned a lot about supplements and nutrients. She also spent years teaching me about the chakra system, the wheels of light we carry in our energetic beings. She taught me that until I mastered my emotional body, it would always master me. So much of my life changed during this time that it was often hard to believe it was still me—in a good way, of course.

Because of her teachings, I could finally understand why when my good friend Minx Boren had her blood tested, it could show that she was twenty-five years younger than she really was. When I met her, Minx had nothing in her refrigerator that I was familiar with. I used to laugh and joke with her about it, when all the time the joke was on me. This was before I was awake, yet I was intelligent enough to know I wanted to remain forever young like her. She was the perfect example of someone who never wronged me. She just kept seeing me become different. From the wisdom of Berenice Andrews, I became a person who ate the way Minx did and was into nutrition as she was. In order to get where we want to be, we must be willing to become what we have not been.

I then prayed for the next healer to come, and a few months later I got a call at the Unity Campus stating that a healer had received a divine message that she was to come from Singapore to St. Petersburg, and she did not know why, but she knew there was a reason. She was told there was a person she would be working on. She worked with me, along with many others, for almost a year, clearing energies of my past and supporting me in truly aligning with my life purpose. It was intense work, and I would recommend it only to people who are serious about changing their energy so their lives will change. My life changed dramatically while we worked together. Guruji Sri Sri Poonamji is the noted guru of Divine Bliss International, and she blessed my life and changed my energy forever.

I also discovered a light worker, Marilyn Gail Rodack, who truly is connected to another dimension, and she totally transformed my core of light so that at times I feel like I am dazzling and sparkling all over. Marilyn transforms people's lives by supporting their light, energy, and inner empowerment. She has the immense gift as a healer to remove the weariness in a person's physical and mental bodies. I feel younger now than I felt in my twenties. She was able to show me what I have always known: that we are able to become younger as we let go of life's weariness and step more and more into the lightness of who we are.

I had been praying for another advance in my abilities, and she was introduced to me by my friend Robert. The first time she met me, Marilyn told me that I was walking around with a straitjacket on and that it had aged me and brought me to a place of weariness.

I had spent so much of my life people-pleasing from my dramatic childhood, carrying old pain around like the bag of rags carried by the beggar and wanting to be accepted, that I had conformed way too many times. At first I did not want to agree with her, because by that time I had shifted a great deal in my life, yet deep down I knew she was right. So much of this stuff is often so deep that we cannot get to it on our own, and we will always have the right healers to guide us if we are open and receptive to allowing ourselves to change.

We can always feel the call in our hearts to grow into more of our possibilities. First we do this by changing our thinking, and second, we shed what no longer belongs in our lives. Then we work from an energy level, which exceeds the intellectual level. Change your energy by opening your heart, and your mind will truly follow.

So many of us have been living our lives in a straitjacket, covering up and being pinned in rather than truly expressing who we are inside. We are not truly listening to our bodies with an open heart. As you renew your mind, open your heart, and you will call in or pray the right healers and ideas into your life, which will give you a new road map to help you find your way toward your magnificence. Always take to prayer the advice that is offered and see if the person talking is the same person in his or her walking.

I have always liked what Wayne Dyer says: "You'll see it when you believe it." I like to say, "A change in heart brings a new start."

I always wanted to meet Sai Baba of India, but I kept putting it off. I kept saying that there would be a better time, but the time did not come. Sai Baba made his transition before I could meet him.

When I was in my twenties, I had watched the video about Sai Baba doing surgery on people, and I read a number of books about him, so when I heard about John of God three times and his incredible ability to allow miracles to happen through him, I was excited to go see him. John of God is an amazing miracle worker noted for claims of healing by Wayne Dyer, Edwene Gaines, Ernie Chu, and thousands of others throughout the world. You may have seen John of God on *The Oprah Winfrey Show*, because she featured him on more than one occasion. You cannot go to Abadiania in Brazil and not have your energy changed. I have never experienced anything like this in my life. People travel to this small town from all over the world. Some of them do so as a last hope; some people have ailments you can see, like large tumors or nonworking limbs, whereas others have issues hidden from the eyes of others.

I was there to express more energy and vitality and to seek support for my message to reach more than a few thousand people, and clearly I was granted my desires. I also received blessings by bringing eight dogs back from Brazil, as I noted earlier, which led to my founding the Sofi Project.

I have been blessed with true teachers and true healers. My seventh-grade teacher, Johanna "Cookie" McMullan Smith, and my ministerial teachers, Bill and Lisa Taliaferro have been significant healers for me, and I am so humbly grateful for their amazing talents and skills. I am very discerning about who works on my body and for what reason. I am past wanting to be someone's experiment. I want only balanced, emotionally stable people to do energy work on my body, for they transfer those energies into me. A true teacher does not train you to do a program so that you become a miniature version of him or her; a true teacher shares his or her knowledge and healing skills with you so you can become the true you.

I have also had a number of teachers who taught me by example how I did *not* want to be, and I could not put a money value on those lessons. I saw how these people acted with others, and I knew I longed to be different from that. A good teacher can change you through negative example as well as through positive example.

I remember Donna Eden, an amazing being who teaches energy medicine. The first time she met me, she said, "You are an energy healer, aren't you?" Donna teaches true techniques and applications that I have been using for many years. For instance, by example she taught me that people who give energy benefit just as much as the people receiving the energy, for the vibration must come through the givers in order to get through to whomever they are giving it to. I have been using an exercise she taught me before my speaking engagements, and the results have been beyond measure. If you haven't heard of her and you are ready for your energy to change in your body so your life will change, she would be an excellent model and teacher for you to have.

Of course, being a healer and a revealer does not mean being all things to all people. It means being an example of the creative life force, being so impassioned and energized that people believe they have the same potential—not to be more like the healer, but to be totally awake and alive as themselves.

We must integrate our inner saboteur and make peace with it in order to step into our destined magnificence. The spiritual warrior ultimately can and will win, yet you must be willing to go to the depths of your soul if you truly long to discover the holy grail.

Key Energy Thoughts

In this section I'd like to share some key thoughts that have shifted my energy.

As long as you believe you are the producer of your own energy, you will always be tired and weary and feel there is never enough. You do, of course, play a significant role in your energy by getting proper rest and nutrition, but you are not the producer of your own vibrant energy any more than you had to think about breathing today before you took your first breath. You can work with healers to increase your light and your essence, yet your energy comes from Spirit. What a joy to awaken into a new day and hear all the creatures on the planet singing with enthusiasm. It's a brand-new day. My energy only increases, for I know I am a catalyst of energy rather than the sole producer of it.

I do not belong to any clubs or groups or have friendships in which people sit around and lick their wounds all day talking about how tired they are, how busy they are, and that they don't know how they do it because there just aren't enough hours in the day. Grow up! Wake up! There have always been twenty-four hours in a day. This is another way in which the emotional body sabotages potentially great people. Their daily prayer becomes "Yea, though I walk through the land of 'there is not enough'—not enough time, not enough help, and not enough money." Life is put on hold until retirement. People who put their good on hold until they grant themselves permission to retire hardly ever live to see those moments become reality. These types of prolonged moments of living are energy zappers. They drain the energy right out of your body and take you from being an ageless spirit to being old and weary.

You are not given a weekly energy ration. None of us go through a line on Sunday afternoon to receive the energy that will get us through the week. If we use a lot of energy on Monday, we do not have to be careful what we do for the remainder of the week. This type of behavior is self-programming and self-limiting. Yet people seem to do it all the time. Many people start the week deciding in the beginning how exhausted they are going to be by Friday, and they become a self-fulfilling prophecy. Energy is now, and it is in the now that it replenishes itself.

What matters is not *what* we are doing but the *energy behind* what we are doing. We are all ready for ideas that give us results. We say,

"Show me a vibration that proves to me that the joy of eating a carrot made it all worthwhile." Energy is magnetic, and people ought to be able to see it by the way a story lives within them.

People through the years have watched me give my time, talent, and treasures to my little six-pound Yorkies, and they often ask me how I can give so much energy to a dog. I usually say, "I am not giving energy to a dog; I am giving energy to life. When you love and give your energy to something, you are not depleted, you are blessed." I could be giving the energy to anything and be receiving as much in return. What matters is not what you give your energy to but how you feel about what you give your energy to. And remember, giving energy to people and other living things gives us energy back.

A thriving life requires quiet time, solitude, and self-care. This rejuvenates the spirit and totally restores the soul. If you want a biblical verse that proves it, there is "he maketh me to lie down in green pastures, he leadeth me beside the still waters." And then what? "He restoreth my soul" (Psalms 23:2–3).

Most people read this and think it refers to when they die, yet for me Psalm 23 is filled with ways in which to truly live. I have used it many times for memorials because I also know that where the dead are going, they are still living, and some of them will be surprised to see that they took themselves to their new destination.

Even if you are currently dying a physical death or know someone who is, remember that it takes energy to walk out of your body. Energy is how we got here, and energy is how we will leave here. If you are feeling disconnected and drained, change your energy, and your life will change. Remember, you are little cups of God, and just as all of nature around you is thriving, so can you thrive. It is your birthright.

If you have been feeling disconnected and drained and want to be impassioned and energized, this is the moment of your new beginning. Declare and affirm this to your energy field: I am ready to stop dying a little every day and start waking up. I am ready to be impassioned and energized.

Your dreams are waiting on you to come true; discover the true you, and they will be found. Find yourself—*you* are the one you have been waiting for.

On behalf of all living things on our planet that desire to be impassioned and energized, thank you for waking up.

Ideas to Process and Integrate

You must change more than your thinking. You must open your heart.
You are the one you have been waiting for.

What new "aha" moment have you experienced, and what changes are you willing to make? You will never move forward by repeating what is in back of you. The people in your huddle are comfortable with you staying the same. When you change, the whole game plan can change.

Too much education and not enough integration is one reason we have not helped the self in the self-help world. We haven't gone deep enough to truly integrate what we have intellectually learned.

What areas in your life do you know better but haven't shown better? Would you be willing to make a change or two for thirty days? If so, what are they?

I have learned to embody the truth from the energy of an open heart.
A change in heart brings a new start.

In what ways are you ready for a new start? Write in your journal any information in this chapter that spoke to you.

EPILOGUE

❦

The Open Heart

Thank you for coming on this journey with me through these eight steps to stop dying every day and start living awake and present. My goal is for you to learn new tools and practices, to find new symbols, to rewrite your story, and to find your unique one-and-only creation story.

When Did You Die? is actually a metaphor for how to open your heart. The little deaths we feel every day lead to a tightened heart, and the way to true bliss and to the riches given to us is through an open heart.

I had to learn I was dying a bit every day before I could find how to embody the truth with an open heart—the only way to feeling, to loving, and to giving beyond what I ever knew I could feel, love, and give. This is the essence of what it means to be both human and divine. This is not about being a victim or taking on responsibility that is not ours; this is the way to reach the well of unconditional love deep inside every one of us. Therein lies the treasure.

For you, dear reader, I wish you and grant you, should you so desire, the gift of an open heart. Mine was closed for years; it had turned to stone and wouldn't soften. It is not in the divine plan to greet each day where we feel bitterness or regret. We are meant to face each day with awe and wonder, and to embrace each other as the divine beings that we are, sharing our eternal journey.

May all that I have shared with you in this book move you forward—to more love, more self-worth, more dreams to come true, and more you! And remember, you are the one who is waiting for you, to embrace every living creature with your heart wide open.

ABOUT THE AUTHOR

ebel, renegade, and resurrected a thousand times, **Temple Hayes** is a prophet and mystic for our time. Raised in South Carolina, she was born to question everything, including her sexual identity. She turned to a new understanding of Spirit to pull her from the car wrecks of alcohol addiction and through a hundred different fears. Firm in her conviction that the Creator loves you as you are and wants to have a conversation, Temple offers practical tools and pithy realizations to jump-start all who die a little bit every day and fast-forward to impassioned and energized living. A practicing shaman, Temple is a catalyst for turning lingering sorrows into brighter tomorrows and restoring all parts of our soul.

The spiritual leader at Unity Campus in St. Petersburg, Florida, Temple is an internationally recognized leader and serves on the Leadership Council of the Association of Global New Thought. She is featured each week on the popular radio show *The Intentional Spirit*. She is the author of *How to Speak Unity* (DeVorss) and *The Right to Be You* (Temple Hayes Ministries) and the founder of Life Rights, a nonprofit organization dedicated to the right of all to live the life of their intention in freedom and peace.

For more information, visit *www.templehayes.com*.